The Internet and the Language Classroom

CAMBRIDGE HANDBOOKS FOR LANGUAGE TEACHERS

This is a series of practical guides for teachers of English and other languages. Illustrative examples are usually drawn from the field of English as a foreign or second language, but the ideas and techniques described can equally well be used in the teaching of any language.

In this series:

Drama Techniques in Language Learning – A resource book of communication activities for language teachers *by Alan Maley and Alan Duff*

Games for Language Learning
by Andrew Wright, David Betteridge and Michael Buckby

Discussions that Work – Task-centred fluency practice *by Penny Ur*

Once Upon a Time – Using stories in the language classroom
by John Morgan and Mario Rinvolucri

Teaching Listening Comprehension – *by Penny Ur*

Keep talking – Communicative fluency activities for language teaching
by Friederike Klippel

Working with Words – A guide to teaching and learning vocabulary
by Ruth Gairns and Stuart Redman

Testing Spoken English – A handbook of oral testing techniques
by Nic Underhill

Literature in the Language Classroom – A resource book of ideas and activities
by Joanne Collie and Stephen Slater

Dictation – New methods, new possibilities *by Paul Davis and Mario Rinvolucri*

Grammar Practice Activities – A practical guide for teachers *by Penny Ur*

Testing for Language Teachers – *by Arthur Hughes*

Pictures for Language Learning – *by Andrew Wright*

Five-Minute Activities – A resource book of short activities
by Penny Ur and Andrew Wright

The Standby Book – Activities for the language classroom *edited by Seth Lindstromberg*

Lessons from Nothing – Activities for language teaching with limited time and resources *by Bruce Marsland*

Beginning to Write – Writing activities for elementary and intermediate learners
by Arthur Brookes and Peter Grundy

Ways of Doing – Students explore their everyday and classroom processes
by Paul Davis, Barbara Garside and Mario Rinvolucri

Using Newspapers in the Classroom – *by Paul Sanderson*

Teaching Adult Second Language Learners – *by Heather McKay and Abigail Tom*

Teaching English Spelling – A practical guide *by Ruth Shemesh and Sheila Waller*

Using Folktales – *by Eric Taylor*

Personalizing Language Learning – Personalized language learning activities
by Griff Griffiths and Kathryn Keohane

Teach Business English – A comprehensive introduction to business English
by Sylvie Donna

Learner Autonomy – A guide to activities which encourage learner responsibility
by Ágota Scharle and Anita Szabó

The Internet and the Language Classroom – Practical classroom activities and projects
by Gavin Dudeney

The Internet and the Language Classroom

Gavin Dudeney

CAMBRIDGE
UNIVERSITY PRESS

PUBLISHED BY THE PRESS SYNDICATE OF THE UNIVERSITY OF CAMBRIDGE
The Pitt Building, Trumpington Street, Cambridge, United Kingdom

CAMBRIDGE UNIVERSITY PRESS
The Edinburgh Building, Cambridge CB2 2RU, UK
40 West 20th Street, New York, NY 10011–4211, USA
10 Stamford Road, Oakleigh, VIC 3166, Australia
Ruiz de Alarcón 13, 28014 Madrid, Spain
Dock House, The Waterfront, Cape Town 8001, South Africa

http://www.cambridge.org

First published 2000
Reprinted 2001

Printed in the United Kingdom at the University Press, Cambridge

Typeface: MT Sabon 10½/12   *System:* QuarkXPress™ [SE]

A catalogue record for this book is available from the British Library

Library of Congress Cataloging-in-Publication Data

Dudeney, Gavin, 1964–
     The internet and the language classroom / Gavin Dudeney.
         p.   cm. – (Cambridge handbooks for language teachers)
     Includes bibliographical references and index.
     ISBN 0-521-80365-9 – ISBN 0-521-78373-9 (pbk.)
         1. Language and languages–Study and teaching–Computer network resources.
     2. Internet in education. I. Title. II. Series.

     P53.285.D83 2000
     418'.00285'4678–dc21   00-048626

ISBN 0 521 78373 9 paperback

45093761

Contents

Acknowledgements   viii
Overview   ix
Introduction   1

1   **Guidelines**   3
  1.0   The World Wide Web   3
  1.1   Website FAQs   8
  1.2   Email   10
  1.3   Email FAQs   16
  1.4   Searching the Internet   17
  1.5   Search FAQs   28
  1.6   The Internet as resource bank   28
  1.7   The Internet as a classroom tool   29

2   **Activities**   37
  2.0   Activities by level   37
  2.0.1   Activities by theme   38
  2.1   Introduction to the Net I   39
  2.2   Introduction to the Net II   41
  2.3   Giving advice   43
  2.4   I've always wondered . . .   44
  2.5   A song class   46
  2.6   20th century news   48
  2.7   Heroes hall of fame   49
  2.8   Celebrity dinner party   51
  2.9   The weather   53
  2.10   Strange news   54
  2.11   Making the news   55
  2.12   Film reviews   57
  2.13   Square eyes   59
  2.14   Eco-tourism   61
  2.15   A little *Je ne sais quoi*   62
  2.16   The same language?   64
  2.17   A good book   66
  2.18   Ladies and gentlemen . . . The Beatles   68

Contents

2.19   Mystery postcards   69
2.20   A terrible holiday   71
2.21   A new logo   73
2.22   Written in the stars   74
2.23   People watching   76
2.24   Get a job   77
2.25   Cooking with kids   79
2.26   Playing it safe   81
2.27   Olympic Games   82
2.28   The London sightseeing tour   84
2.29   What's the time?   85
2.30   Dream holiday   87
2.31   A night at the movies   88
2.32   Classified ads   91
2.33   Finding a flat   92
2.34   Suits you   93
2.35   A fine day out   95
2.36   But is it art?   97
2.37   Puzzlemaker   98
2.38   Holiday posters   100
2.39   Nice day today   101
2.40   Disaster area   103
2.41   Kids make the news   105
2.42   It's a mystery   106
2.43   Australian wildlife   108
2.44   Theme park   109
2.45   Computer detectives   110
2.46   Who said that . . .?   112
2.47   Waving the flag   113
2.48   Dream houses   115
2.49   Net research   117
2.50   What do you think of . . .?   118
2.51   Survival   120
2.52   Teen spirit   122
2.53   What's in a name?   123
2.54   Discoveries and inventions   125
2.55   Reviewing a website   126

3   Projects   128
3.0   Email penpal exchanges   128
3.1   Writing projects   133
3.2   Web-based projects   134

4 **Advanced Net 148**
    4.0   Browser enhancements   148
    4.1   Talking to other teachers – mailing lists   150
    4.2   Listserv FAQs   155
    4.3   Online chat   156
    4.4   Browser caching   161

5 **FAQs 162**
    5.0   Connecting to the Internet   162
    5.1   Internet terminology   163
    5.2   Selected websites   165
    5.3   Starting a website review file   170
    5.4   Publishing student material   172

Recommended resources   174
Index   175

Acknowledgements

This book is dedicated to my wife Marta and my parents Peter and Tess.

This book would not have been possible without the help, support and suggestions of friends and colleagues at International House Barcelona and IH Net Languages who helped with initial reading and tidying up.

Many thanks too, to Penny Ur and Jayshree Ramsurun for their insightful editing and Jane Clifford at CUP for support throughout and making it happen.

The Brief history of the Web activity in Activity 2.1 was first suggested to me by David Hunter. Activity 2.19 was first suggested to me by Paul Henderson, a former colleague. Activity 2.53 was first suggested to me by Robert Campbell of iT's Magazine.

The author and publishers are grateful to the following for permission to reproduce copyright screenshots. It has not been possible to identify the sources of all material and in such cases the publishers would welcome information from copyright holders.

pp 4, 7, 137, and 160, used by permission from Microsoft Corporation; pp 11 and 12, printed with permission of QUALCOMM Incorporated; pp 17, 18 and 21 reproduced with permission of AltaVista; pp 23 and 25 reproduced with permission of Yahoo! Inc. © 2000 by Yahoo! Inc. YAHOO! and the YAHOO! logo are trademarks of Yahoo! Inc.; pp 156 and 157, permission given by mIRC Co Ltd.

Overview

Guidelines

Here the teacher is introduced to different aspects of the Internet, with a look at software, different modes of communication on the Internet, finding and classifying resources and a brief consideration of the practicalities of the Internet as a resource bank and as a classroom tool. In this part you will learn how to use the World Wide Web and email.

Activities

Activities at all levels, with photocopiable resources and clear instructions on how to make the most of them, covering the basic introductory classes before proceeding through a wide variety of popular themes (e.g. cinema, accommodation, the environment, news and media, etc.) and language points. Many of the activities have sample worksheets and are readily adaptable for most levels. A useful guide at the beginning of this section breaks down these activities by theme and by level.

Projects

This section looks at sample web-based and email projects including an examination of how to create simple web projects, ideas for extended project work and guidelines on how to set up and run global projects such as email and cultural exchanges.

Advanced Net

This section gives helpful advice on how to increase your knowledge and skills on the Internet so you get even more from your online experiences.

FAQs (Frequently Asked Questions)

Here you'll find answers to questions from how to connect to the Internet to where to publish your students' work. A brief guide to the more common Internet terminology and a list of useful websites appear here. Also included are a sample website review form and a release form for use with student work to be published on the Internet.

It should be noted that the Internet is in a constant state of change, and that while all the practical activities have been based around websites with a good degree of stability, it is possible that some sites mentioned may have changed or ceased to be available by the time you read this. This said, the Internet is such an enormous resource, that any website which suffers this fate will surely be replaced by half a dozen more of similar or better quality and content.

Regular updates to this book – and extra material – can be found at the accompanying website: http://www.cambridge.org/elt/chlt/internet

Introduction

The Internet, often abbreviated to the Net, has often been described as the biggest communications revolution since the advent of the printed book, yet up until not too long ago it was a secretive field enjoyed – and jealously guarded – by a few select individuals. These days, however, things have changed for the better, and the Net is now a thriving community with many millions of people exchanging information, ideas and opinions. The development of easier connections, more user-friendly software (the programs which computers use, such as word processors, Internet web browsers, etc.) and cheaper access has opened up the 'information superhighway' to everyone, from young children – at home and at school – to professionals in all fields and walks of life.

For language teachers, involved in the communication process on a very basic level, it is the perfect medium. Language teachers are constantly on the lookout for quality, authentic teaching material. Almost all the teachers I know are no longer able to simply read a book or a magazine, listen to a song or watch a film or television programme without considering the *material's* possible value for exploitation in the classroom. We spend hours collecting leaflets and menus, handouts in the street and free magazines from street stands, and buying foreign language newspapers and magazines (often at great personal expense).

Now, all this material is quickly, cheaply and readily available from the comfort of our desks or homes. To the busy teacher the Internet can be an infinite resource file of texts, visual stimuli, listening material, vocabulary, information, video files, live TV and radio, newspapers from around the world … The list is endless.

And, of course, it's not merely a source of authentic material in English, but also home to encyclopaedic information about all sorts of topics you may want to engage with in the classroom, and of professional knowledge for teachers: bibliographies, chat groups, articles, courses and conferences.

Yet despite all this, every day I am witness to comments along the lines of 'I finally got connected, but I just can't find anything', or 'I spent four hours looking round and didn't see a single good site', or even 'I searched for material on Australia, but there were over seven million pages and I just didn't know where to start'.

1

This book is the result of these typical scenarios in the life of a busy language teacher and an attempt to bring a bit of focus, structure and meaning to the Internet – to help teachers get the most from this exhilarating medium. The different sections look at the skills and resources needed to exploit the Internet to the full – both as a resource for teachers, and as an integral part of classroom activity.

There are various tips, and quick 'hands on' activities in most of the sections of this book. Watch out for these symbols as you read:

TIP ☑   **HANDS ON** ✉

This book includes many suggestions to download, print out and reuse text and graphics from the Net. It is, however, your own responsibility to ensure that any material you find and wish to reuse is free from copyright. Most sites make clear whether or not you have free licence with their material. If in doubt, use the email address to ask them. There is usually one given.

Teachers have a responsibility for child protection, particularly when teaching younger learners. When using the Internet, care should be taken about both the kind of material learners have access to and the type of personal information they publish online.

1 Guidelines

The Internet is often used as a term to describe the World Wide Web. In fact, the World Wide Web is just one part of this multi-faceted communication medium which takes in anything from simple text communication by email, to video-conferencing (a two-way conversation using a small video camera and a microphone) with high-quality sound and video.

There are hundreds of different ways of communicating by means of an Internet connection, but you can get nearly everything you want from the Internet with just two things: the World Wide Web and email. Once you have learnt these two sides of the Net, you will be fully prepared to make good and full use of all the material in this book. And when everything is under control, you can move onto some of the more advanced tips and techniques introduced in *Section 4 Advanced Net*.

1.0 The World Wide Web

> **TIP** ☑
>
> Depending on where you are in the world, your access to the Internet will be faster at certain times of the day. In Barcelona, access is very quick until about 2 pm and then gets gradually slower. This is due to the fact that Internet use in the States is heavier – because of the time difference – at that time of the day. When I'm using the Net in the morning, most people in the States are sleeping.

The World Wide Web (otherwise known as the Web or WWW) is the medium of choice for both new and experienced users on the Net, and for good reasons: it's visually attractive, easy-to-use, easy-to-understand, and manages to combine many other Internet-based forms of communication into a single manageable package.

Most modern computers already come equipped with the tools needed to connect to the Internet. All you need are a modem, a telephone line (or, for a faster connection, an ISDN adapter card and ISDN phone line) and an

Internet service provider. A modem is a piece of machinery inside the computer which enables your computer to 'talk' to other computers via a standard telephone line. An Internet service provider (ISP) is a company which has large and extremely powerful computers permanently connected to the Internet. When you connect to the Internet with your computer, you are making a phone call to your ISP: once linked to your ISP, you can use its computer to gain access to all the other computers connected to the Internet. Most Internet magazines these days have plenty of information about ISPs and how to get connected.

To view and interact with the Web, you use a Web browser. This is a piece of software which helps you move around the Web and displays the information you are interested in. There are many different browsers, but the two most popular are: Netscape Communicator (Netscape) and Microsoft Internet Explorer (Explorer). Both of these programs are free, and available for both Macintosh computers and the various versions of Windows.

In the picture below, you can see the Microsoft Internet Explorer browser with most of the major features explained. Netscape's Communicator is very similar. All the illustrations in this book show Microsoft's Internet Explorer. Where there is a major difference between the two, this will be explained.

The **Back** and **Forward** Buttons let you move between webpages you have visited

The **Favorites** button shows you a list of all the websites you have saved.

The **History** button allows you to view and go back to the pages you have visited recently.

The **Print** button prints what you can see on screen.

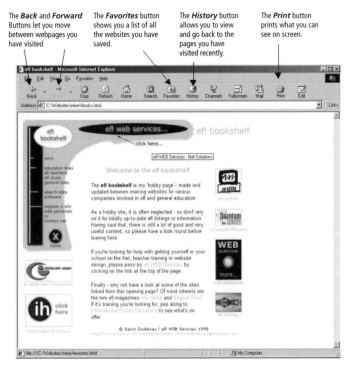

If you are connected to the Internet, you can get either browser free of charge. To get Internet Explorer, go to http://www.microsoft.com/ie/download, to get Netscape Communicator, visit the Netscape site at http://www.netscape.com/download/index.html If you are not connected to the Internet yet, the best way to get these browsers is to buy an Internet magazine with a cover-mounted CD-ROM – they are nearly always included free. Even if you are connected, it's easier and quicker to install them from a CD as the download times for big programs such as web browsers can be long and expensive.

The Web is simply a collection of screens of information (known as webpages) which reside on many thousands of computers around the world, all of which are permanently connected to the Internet. These pages are all linked together, or classified in various directories and search catalogues.

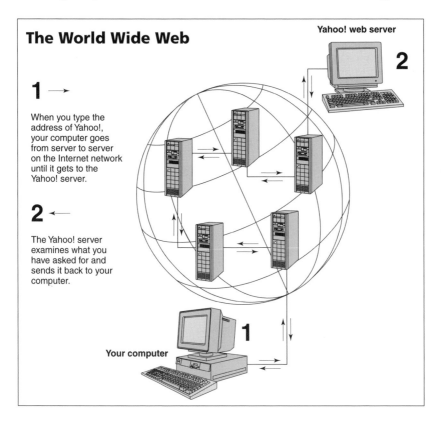

The World Wide Web

Yahoo! web server

1 →

When you type the address of Yahoo!, your computer goes from server to server on the Internet network until it gets to the Yahoo! server.

2 ←

The Yahoo! server examines what you have asked for and sends it back to your computer.

Your computer

When we visit one of these computers and view something there, we are looking at a website – a collection of webpages built around a common theme – for as long as we are connected. A website can range from a simple page or screen (perhaps an advertisement for, or review of, a book) to an enormous collection of pages (maybe a publishing company's entire book catalogue).

Your first visit

Once you are connected to the Web (see the **FAQs** section for more advice on connecting to the Internet) and you have your browser installed, you will be ready to start visiting websites. To do this, all you have to do is click once inside the white box at the top of your browser window, next to where it says *Address* (Explorer) or *Location* (Netscape) and type the address of a web page: http://www.yahoo.com This might look indecipherable, but in fact it has a very simple and logical structure:

http:// tells you it's a webpage

www.yahoo.com a webpage address – com usually stands for commercial (as does the abbreviation co)

TIP ☑

You must make sure you type Internet addresses exactly as they appear. If you don't, you won't get where you want to go.

When you have typed the address, press *Enter* on the keyboard and wait a few seconds. This particular example will take you to Yahoo! – a directory of websites around the world. Here's another example: http://www.telegraph.co.uk This one will take you to the Electronic Telegraph, the Web-based version of the British newspaper *The Daily Telegraph*. Again, you can tell it's a webpage – from the http:// part, and that it's a commercial concern (.co), but you also have the added information which tells you it's based in the United Kingdom (.uk).

Let's try http://www.ihes.com/bcn/ – the address of the International House Barcelona homepage. (I made the page, so I know where everything is!) When you have typed the address, press *Enter* on your keyboard and wait for your computer to find the information you have asked for. When the page appears in your browser window, you will see a combination of text and images:

A homepage is the opening page of a website – rather like the front door to a large house. When you get inside, you can decide which page you want to visit first by clicking on the links you find.

A link is a word or phrase – or sometimes an image – which is connected to another part of the website using a system called hypertext. These links are usually in a different colour from the rest of the text (mostly blue and underlined – but not always) and provide the structure of a website, allowing the user to decide which parts of the site they want to visit.

TIP ☑

Move your mouse over the text and images on a webpage and you will find the cursor sometimes changes shape into a pointing finger. This indicates a hyperlink or connection to another page. Click on the link and you will be taken to that page. Try it on the page above.

Notice how the International House page runs off the bottom of the screen. You can use the scroll bar on the right hand side of the browser window (or the *Page Down* and *Page Up* keys) to move down and back up the page. Other useful keys for those who prefer keyboards are *Home* – which takes you to the top of a webpage and *End* – which takes you to the bottom.

When you've finished looking at the page, press the *Back* button at the top of the screen on the left, to return to the page before. Now try pressing the *Forward* button – no prizes for guessing what it does.

Maybe you've decided that this page could be useful to you later, but how are you going to remember the address? The simple answer is that you bookmark it, like you would an interesting passage in a book. In Netscape, click on the *Bookmarks* button and choose the *Add bookmark* option – the address will be added to your bookmarks and next time you want to visit this site, you'll simply have to click on the *Bookmarks* button and then click on the name of the site. In Explorer, bookmarks are called *Favorites* and you can create new ones by clicking on the *Favorites* button and choosing the *Add to Favorites* option.

Finally, you might think that this site is worth printing out and sharing with other teachers where you work, or taking to class. Nothing could be simpler – click on the *Print* button and the page will be printed automatically.

You've now learnt almost all you need to know about getting round the Web.

HANDS ON

Use the list of addresses in the **FAQs** section at the back of the book to practise visiting and moving around websites. Don't forget to add any interesting ones to your *Bookmarks* or *Favorites*. Print out a few to share with colleagues.

1.1 Website FAQs:

This is the first of many Frequently Asked Questions (FAQs) lists in this book. FAQs are often used on websites and discussion lists and their purpose is to answer all the common questions one might ask on a first visit. They are also there to save time for the person who made the website or administers the discussion list!

I'M TRYING TO VISIT A WEBSITE, BUT NOTHING'S HAPPENING. WHAT'S WRONG?

Websites can sometimes be unobtainable temporarily for various reasons. If you try to get to a site and it just won't open – or you get a screen with an error message, first check that you have got the address right. If it still won't open you should try again later. Although some websites do disappear for ever, most of them are fairly reliable.

I CLICKED ON A LINK, BUT IT'S GOING SO SLOWLY. WHAT'S THE PROBLEM?

Connections to the Internet can vary in speed during the day. If a website appears to be taking a long time to get to you, try clicking the *Stop* button on your browser and then clicking the link again. It's not the sort of thing that immediately occurs to most people, but it often works. If this doesn't solve the problem, stop and try again later.

I'VE FOUND A GREAT WEBPAGE – HOW DO I PRINT IT?

You can print part of a website by choosing the *Print* option from the file menu and specifying which pages you want to print. If a website is made with frames (multiple windows on the screen) you must first click inside the frame you want to print before choosing the print command.

WHICH IS BETTER – NETSCAPE OR EXPLORER?

Everyone has an opinion on which is the best browser. My advice is to choose one and stick to it. They both do the same things and using one makes it easier to keep track of your *Bookmarks* or *Favorites*.

I'D LIKE TO USE PART OF A WEBPAGE FOR A WORKSHEET. HOW DO I DO THAT?

If you are used to working with Word 97 or similar, you'll find that you can do a lot of work with the two programs open at the same time. Text on a webpage behaves the same as text in a word processor. You can click and drag out a selection of text on a webpage and copy it, then paste it into a word processor document. This is useful for just printing the text from a page rather than all the images and advertisements, for preparing worksheets from webpages, etc.

1.2 Email

Once you have had some practice and gained some experience with the Web it's time to move on to look at email. Email is, for many reasons, the most used tool on the Internet: it's easy to use, it's cheap, fast and reliable.

Of course, you can use email directly from your browser (Netscape or Explorer), but I really would recommend having a dedicated email program. There are many reasons for wanting to do this, but the most important one is that it will work more quickly and more efficiently than the mail service of a browser and is much more versatile.

TIP ☑

It is worth noting here that as the Internet gains ground in everyday life, the terminology changes. Along with many other people, I use email as one word, but it is still quite common to see it written 'e-mail' – as it was spelt when it was first invented: a short way of saying 'electronic mail'.

Increasingly, the word 'email' is used – and almost universally accepted – as a verb and a countable noun ('I'll email you tomorrow'; 'I just got an email from my cousin'.).

There are many popular email programs, and in the end it's a question of personal preference. The most popular programs are Eudora and Outlook Express. In this book I'll be looking at Eudora, but most of the functions and options are the same in other email packages.

In the picture opposite, you can see the two boxes marked *In* (where messages sent to you arrive) and *Out* (where messages you send go) – there are messages in each box in this example. Other mailboxes include *Trash* (where deleted messages go) and any personalised ones you create for filing messages you want to keep. (My mailboxes are on the left.)

TIP ☑

Eudora Light is free to download at http://www.qualcomm.com . If you want to use Outlook Express, you should find it already installed on your computer if you have downloaded and installed Internet Explorer or the Microsoft Office software.

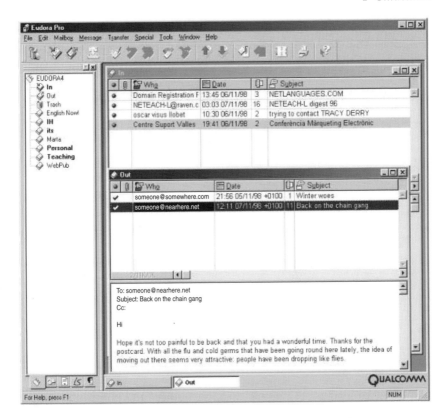

There are normally six steps involved in working with an email program. Most of these steps can be done while you are not connected to the Internet (this is known as working offline). You can read messages sent to you, and write new messages without the need to be connected to the Internet and without running up an enormous phone bill.

Here is what you do:

1 Write new mail messages.
2 Connect to the Net.
3 Send the messages and check for new mail.
4 Disconnect from the Net.
5 Read new mail.
6 Reply to mail. (Then continue from Step 1 above.)

To write a message, click on the menu option called *Message* at the top of the screen and then click on *New Message* (keyboard users do Ctrl + N). When you do this, the window below appears:

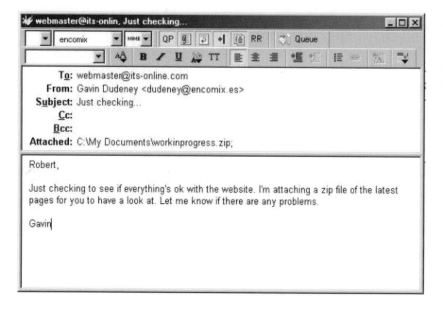

In order to send a message successfully, you need to know the address of the person you are sending to. Eudora will automatically put your name and email address in the *From* field. It's customary to put a *Subject* line so that the person who receives it has an idea of what it's about.

TIP ☑

Because email addresses are difficult to remember, Eudora has a feature called *Nicknames*. When you receive a message from someone you think you'll want to write to in the future, click on *Special* and choose *Make Nickname* to have Eudora remember the name and address of the person. Now when you want to write to them, click on *Message* and go to *New Message To* and choose a person from the list which appears.

Email messages are simply text documents which can be sent over the Net. They are usually small and written in a 'shorthand' form, ignoring the normal conventions of written language. Essentially this means that they are written in informal language and there is no need to include the 'extras' of ordinary letters such as dates, addresses or formal greetings. It is not uncommon, for example, to see plenty of abbreviations which are particular to this medium: 'u' for 'you', 'r' for 'are', and the longer ones such as IMHO (in my humble opinion), FYI (for your information) and BTW (by the way). These are designed to make email quicker to write, and, to some extent, help express feelings and emotions which might otherwise be lost to the reader, or require far more words to communicate.

To write to someone, all you have to do is know their address. When you've finished writing your message, click the *Queue* button. The message will be closed and saved in the *Outbox* of Eudora, with a letter *Q* next to it. Now connect up to the Internet and click on *File* and go to *Send Queued Messages*. Your message will be sent, and the *Q* next to it will change to a ✓ or *S* (depending on the version you are using).

TIP ☑

You have to be very careful when you are writing down email addresses, or typing them into the address field of a new email message you are about to send. One small mistake and the message will be returned to you. This phenomenon is known as bouncing, and it takes up a lot of Internet resources every day. You can do your bit to make the Internet a faster and more efficient place by being careful when sending mail.

To collect your mail, connect to the Internet, and click on *File* and go to *Check Mail*. When you do this, the messages are removed from your service provider's machine and moved to your machine, where they land in the *Inbox*. Once you've collected your message you can go offline and read them (just double click on any message). You may also want to print them using the print icon at the top of the program, delete them (just click once on the message and press the delete key), reply to them by clicking on *Message* and going to *Reply*. Or you may want to file them in another folder.

HANDS ON ✉

Try sending some email now. Open up your email program and send yourself a message (this is a good way to see if your mail program is correctly set up). When you have sent it, wait a couple of minutes and then check to see if you have new mail: your message should come back to you in your Inbox.

Create a new mailbox called Personal (click on *Mailbox* and go to *New*, type Personal and click OK). Notice how the new mailbox appears on the left of the screen. Click on your recently received message, then click *Transfer* and go to *Personal*. Filing your messages is a very good idea, especially if you receive a lot of mail every day.

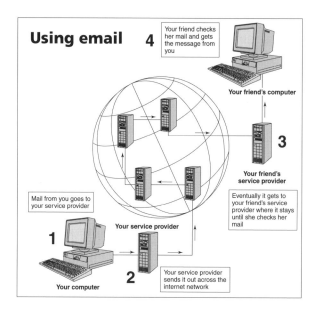

There are rules for email and other forms of written communication on the Internet. Brief messages, shorthand and abbreviations are the order of the day with email. Some people connected to the Net actually pay for the amount of text they receive, so they will thank you for being brief. The other rules are collected together in a set of guidelines known as Netiquette. A few of the more important issues connected with email are covered here, but you can find out all about it at the Netiquette Home Page: http//www.fau.edu/netiquette/net/

TIP ☑

Eudora can automatically add a *signature* to every message you send (e.g. your telephone or fax number, place of work or anything else you want people to know). To create a signature, click *Tools*, go to *Signature* and choose *Standard*. Type what you want people to see. Close the signature box and save the changes.

Email can be used for many purposes, from writing to friends and relatives, to having information sent to you on a regular basis (for example the football results every Monday morning, international currency exchange rates every day or even job openings on a weekly basis), to getting hold of resources (e.g. from a listserv – see *Section 4 Advanced Net*). It can even be used to send and receive other things such as picture files, word processed documents and sound files.

The ability to attach other documents is useful for many things. Imagine you want to apply for a teaching job by email. If you copy your beautifully presented cv into an email message, it will lose all its colour, bold text, underlining, etc. since most email does not really support such options. To send your cv as it is, all you have to do is attach it to your email message – this means that it travels <u>with</u> rather than <u>in</u> your message. In Eudora, click *Message* and go to *Attach File* and then find and double-click on the name of the file you want to send. Now when you queue and send your message, the file will also be sent.

You should be aware that the person who receives your message will need the correct software to open the attached file; if your cv was made with Microsoft Word, for example, the person who receives it will need to have something capable of reading Word documents installed on their computer in order to open it.

TIP ☑

If you're not sure what software the recipient has, the best option is to save any document in Rich Text Format (RTF) – you'll find this in the *Save As ...* dialogue box in programs like Microsoft Word. Just choose the *Save as Type ...* option and change it to RTF. RTF documents can be read by most modern word processors.

HANDS ON 🖅

Send me some mail. Write to webmaster@bcn.ihes.com and tell me how you are getting on with the book so far. I promise to answer. Try copying (Cc) the message to yourself, but please don't send any attachments!

1.3 Email FAQs

I KEEP GETTING 'JUNK' MAIL. WHAT SHOULD I DO?

Eventually you will start to receive advertising and 'make money quick' email messages ('junk' mail). Ignore them. Don't waste more valuable Internet resources by replying to them or forwarding them to friends and colleagues.

SOMEONE HAS SENT ME A VIRUS WARNING BY EMAIL. IS MY COMPUTER IN DANGER?

Don't panic if you receive a virus warning by email. It is impossible (to date) for your computer to be infected by a virus from a simple email message. These warnings travel the Internet constantly and are the bane of experienced users. Again, ignore and delete.

You can, however, get a virus from an attachment if you open the file. If someone you don't know sends you an attachment you're not expecting it's safest to delete it if you have no virus protection software.

TIP ☑

Although most virus warnings sent by email are false alarms and hoaxes, there are ways to pick up viruses over the Internet, so it's worth having up-to-date virus protection on your computer – try Norton AntiVirus or McAfee.

I JUST GOT A VERY ANGRY MESSAGE FROM SOMEONE I WROTE TO. WHAT DID I DO?

There are a number of things which offend experienced users of email – here are some possibilities:

- People you write to cannot see your face, or guess what you are thinking. Perhaps you didn't explain yourself clearly, or something in the document was misunderstood;
- Maybe you didn't include information about who you are and where you're from and consequently the person didn't know who the message was from;
- Did you write in capital LETTERS? – it's the Internet equivalent of shouting and frowned on by most people;
- It's possible you inadvertently sent an attachment along with your message. Unsolicited attachments are guaranteed to make people angry, especially if they pay a lot for their online time. A teacher I know sent a copy of Word

for Windows as an attachment – quite by accident – and was very unpopular for a few days!

- Perhaps you have an enormously long signature at the end of your message and the person is angry about the extra time it took to receive your message.

1.4 Searching the Internet

When first approaching the Web, people often feel as if they are spending a lot of time getting nowhere; clicking on link after link leads to somewhere which has nothing of interest to them, waiting minutes for large images to appear, attempting to visit pages which no longer exist, etc. After a while any normal person would give up and turn to a newspaper. A familiar comment from new users is that 'there is nothing there', which is rather similar to visiting a hypermarket and saying there's nothing to buy. The fact of the matter is that there is plenty to see on the Web, it's just a case of knowing how to find it, or where to look.

A new user will inevitably be led to one of the bigger search engine's sites like Yahoo! (http://www.yahoo.com) or AltaVista (http://www.altavista.com), and will try searching for something they are interested in. This search usually involves typing in a word (e.g. Australia) and hitting the *Submit* button. This is what happens if you do just that at AltaVista.

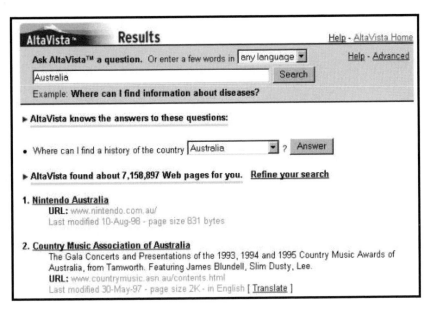

AltaVista has over eight million webpages containing the word 'Australia' in its database. It would be impossible to go through them all looking for something in particular.

Notice how, in the picture, AltaVista tries to guess what you are looking for with the suggested answers (*AltaVista knows the answers to these questions*). You should always look at the suggestions, but don't expect them to be useful.

With a little refinement, e.g. doing a search for "Sydney Opera House Australia", the results are dramatically reduced, and in this case amount to a grand total of ninety pages (try it yourself – one of them takes you to a great photo of the Opera House).

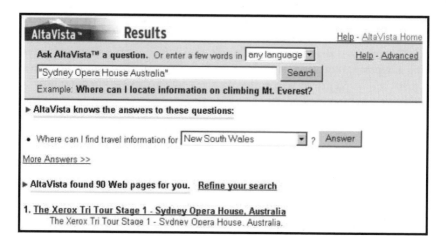

The first results page gives you hypertext links to the first ten pages. Each link has a small summary below it, and additional information such as the date the page was last changed or updated. If you click on one of the links, you should get to a page which has something to do with Sydney Opera House.

If you scroll down to the bottom of the results page, you will see the word *Pages* and the numbers *1, 2, 3,* ... next to it. Clicking on page 2 will take you to the second page of results where you will find links to pages 11–20 of the ninety pages it has found. Eventually, with such small results you should find what you are looking for.

And, every time you actually get to a site you were looking for, use your browser wisely to add the site to your *Bookmarks* (Netscape) or *Favorites* (Explorer). Nothing is more annoying than finding a great site, then forgetting to save a record of its address and having to go through the whole painful process of searching for it again.

I use the word 'painful' with reason: there are no great ways of searching for information on the Web, no guaranteed search processes which will smoothly and quickly take you where you want to go. However, this section of the book will teach you three different ways of searching for resources and hopefully arm you with all the skills you need to find anything you want – albeit with a little trial and error.

Introduction to search types

There are three principal ways of searching the Web: search engines, subject guides and 'real language' search pages.

Search engines allow you to type in words connected with the information you are looking for – these words are then compared with a database of web-pages and their contents. Having matched the search words with pages in the database, the search engine displays a list of documents for you to consult.

TIP ☑

All search sites have help pages – make sure you visit them and find out how they work – five minutes spent doing this will save many hours and ease the frustration of bad search results.

Searching for something on the Web has almost been made more difficult by the proliferation of search sites. But, whichever search you decide to use, here are some questions you should be asking yourself:

- What exactly am I looking for? (webpage, image, etc.);
- Is this a general or specific search? (general searches work best in a subject guide, while specific searches are best left to search engines);
- How much information do I want? (some search engines feature reviews, summary of page content, etc.);
- Can I use the search engine? (some search pages are very difficult to use properly and require a full reading of the help page).

Refining searches using a search engine

As I pointed out in the introduction to this section, visiting a search page on the Web, typing in the word 'Australia' and hitting the *Submit* button will get you a list of over eight million sites to visit. Starting this way leaves the user with a wealth of information, and a potential lifetime of investigation on this one subject alone. However a search can be refined in order to limit the number of page references returned. The answer lies in the shape of 'operators' and punctuation. The next part shows you what these tools are and how they work with AltaVista.

TIP

AltaVista can search for webpages in most languages. If you are looking for resources in a language other than English, try changing the *Any language* menu to the language of your choice.

AND, OR AND NOT

These look for various combinations of search words and operate like this:

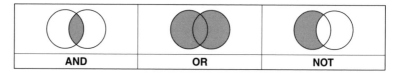

AND (+) looks for documents featuring **all** words in the search entry box; OR looks for documents featuring **any** of the words in the search entry box; NOT (−) looks for documents featuring **some** words, but not others. Therefore a search for *EFL AND London* should take you to sites connected with teaching English as a Foreign Language in London, whereas a search for *EFL NOT London* will find you all the sites on the subject anywhere else in the world. A search done using *EFL OR London* should give you a list of both types of site (and a lot more).

TIP ☑

Some search engines use the words 'AND' and 'NOT', others use the mathematical symbols '+' and '−'. To find out which ones to use on a particular search engine, read the help file.

These three search words can be 'nested' (i.e. combined), providing very close matches: *EFL AND London AND (study OR teach)*. That is if you're looking for information about studying or teaching English in London.

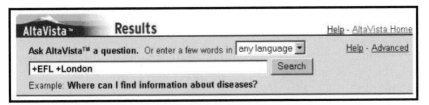

This search will look for pages which have both words on them somewhere.

HANDS ON 🖎

Try going to AltaVista and doing some searches using the options described above. See if you can find the address of my homepage. Gavin isn't a very common name, but you won't want to find all the Gavins, so try: +Gavin +Dudeney

If you don't have too much luck, you'll find the address towards the end of this section of the book.

Note: These search terms are taken from the world of mathematics and are sometimes referred to as Boolean Operators. If you see this term anywhere on the Internet, just think AND, OR and NOT.

NEAR, ADJACENT AND FOLLOWED BY

These look for words which are close to each other in documents. ADJACENT looks for words next to each other, whereas the other two vary in proximity according to the search agent used (usually about ten words either side of each other). Typing in *teach NEAR Paris* will find pages on the Web with content related to teaching in Paris. This is a slightly freer search than one using punctuation (see below), since the two words don't have to be right next to each other for the page to feature in the search results. A page found with the above search might include sentences such as: 'I have always wanted to teach in a school in Paris ...', 'Paris is a wonderful place to teach ...', etc.

Note: These search terms are often called Proximity Operators on the Internet.

PUNCTUATION

Punctuation (as the word is used in the context of a search site) allows the user to look for phrases (or parts of phrases) in Web documents. This is probably the most common way of searching. Punctuation in this context refers to the use of inverted commas.

When you use inverted commas you have to put yourself in the place of the person who wrote the page you are looking for. Let's suppose you are looking for some information about Marilyn Monroe for a class about famous people. If you made a page about her, what would you include? (pictures, biography, filmography, etc.) So, you could start with a search along these lines: "*biography of Marilyn Monroe*". The words have to occur next to each other, and in that order as part of a phrase to score a hit with the search.

TIP ☑

Using inverted commas is one of the best tips to teach your students. One of my students in Barcelona once tried searching for "the Sting's biography", instead of "biography of Sting" – a common mistake for Spanish learners of English. He didn't find anything, but he soon learnt not to make the same mistake in English!

Another useful operator to know about is the asterisk (sometimes referred to as 'truncation' on search sites). This is used to find part of a word, e.g. a search for *car** automatically brings back results for any words which begin with these three letters: car, carting, cartoon, Cartagena, Carmichael, etc.

AltaVista offers two ways to search its database, simple and advanced. Advanced Queries can be very complex, so it's best to check the Advanced Help Pages before using this option.

TIP ☑

AltaVista has a machine translation service which automatically translates webpages between some languages. You can try it by clicking on translate next to any search result address, or by following the translation link from the opening page. It's functional – but don't expect too much.

Search strategies for subject guides

Subject guides have more in common with the index of a book, with information classified by topic and subject. These allow users to browse through lists of sites by subject, in search of something relevant. The main difference between these and search engines is that subject guides are compiled by humans. This has both a positive and negative effect on searches; positive in the respect that the database for the search engine usually only lists top-level documents (homepages) and therefore doesn't take you to the middle of a website; negative in that the database is usually a lot smaller than that of a search engine (humans being slower than machines!). An example of a good subject guide is Yahoo! (http://www.yahoo.com)

TIP ☑

There are many different versions of Yahoo! for different countries. Follow the links from the homepage to the Spanish Yahoo!, the German Yahoo!, the Japanese Yahoo!, etc.

Yahoo! can also be used as a search agent in much the same way as AltaVista – you can use the operators AND and OR, and even quotation marks. However, its real strength lies in its structure: that of a subject guide.

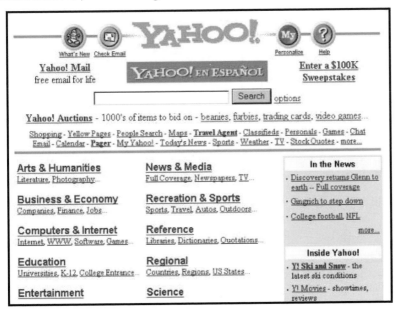

HANDS ON

Visit Yahoo! now and browse some of the sections – try to find webpages connected with your hobbies and interests, or look for information on a famous person. Now try the same thing in AltaVista based on what you have read above. See how quickly you find what you are looking for.

Yahoo! allows users to simply browse through categories and sub-categories, gradually refining a search until the desired results are achieved. A typical search which might take a considerable amount of time on AltaVista can often be a lot quicker through Yahoo!

Searching for resources on Yahoo! can be considered like an inverted pyramid: you start with a wide area of reference and keep refining it and making choices until you get where you want to be. For example, if searching for a biography of Sting for a class on pop music, a typical route might be:

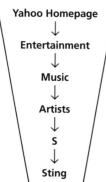

Yahoo Homepage
↓
Entertainment
↓
Music
↓
Artists
↓
S
↓
Sting

Starting at the homepage, first click on the *Music* sub-heading of *Entertainment*. When this page has opened, click on *Artists* and finally *S* to get to a page of links for musical artists whose names begin with that letter.

If you try this particular search, you will find that there are many hundreds of music artists whose names begin with the letter 'S', and this adds up to a long and slow page of search results. A quicker way to get to Sting is to go as far as the *Entertainment-Music-Artists* section of Yahoo! and then type *Sting* in the Search box (see picture opposite).

Now we can search for Sting, but just in this category. This restricts results to Sting the musical artist rather than the other stings (jellyfish, nettle, wasp, bee).

TIP ☑

While writing this I was asked by a colleague to help her find the website of The Scotsman – a newspaper published in Scotland. Here's how the same search works on AltaVista and Yahoo!:

AltaVista

Searching for *The Scotsman* found hundreds of articles quoted by other people from past editions of *The Scotsman*. I vainly tried visiting a few

---

in the hope that one of them would have a link to the newspaper. This was not the case. Back to the search page to try again. Next I tried *title: "The Scotsman"*, but it soon became obvious that the electronic edition had a different name and this wasn't going to work either. This took twenty minutes, so I gave up and turned to Yahoo!

Yahoo!

I followed links through *Regional – Countries – United Kingdom – Scotland – News and Media – Newspapers – The Scotsman*. Six clicks and I was looking at the front page of the newspaper.

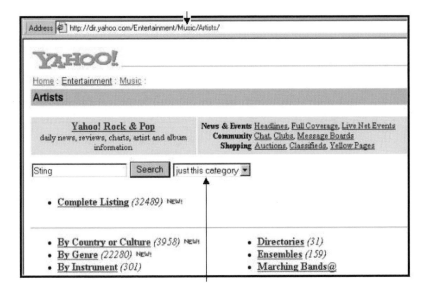

Using 'real language' search sites

Using search facilities like AltaVista and Yahoo! is not for everyone. Even when you know all the different ways of searching, it's sometimes a very time-consuming process to get to what you are actually looking for. Wouldn't it be nice if you could just ask something like 'Where can I find a picture of Sydney Opera House?', as you would if you were asking a colleague.

The answer is that these days you can. All you need to do is Ask Jeeves (http://www.askjeeves.com) and he'll see what he can do for you. Ask Jeeves is a very simple way of searching the Net. You don't have to remember all the punctuation rules of pages like AltaVista and Yahoo! – you just type in a normal question and see what happens.

'Real language' search pages allow the browser to ask a question, then they give suggested answers. These searches are a recent development, so don't expect incredibly precise results all the time.

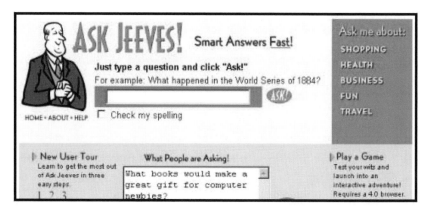

Having said that, if you try it out a few times, you might be surprised at the excellent results you can get. This might all seem very magical, but in actual fact Jeeves is only doing what the other two search engines do, it just does it in a more user-friendly way. Jeeves doesn't actually understand real English, so when you type a question like: "What time is it in Bangkok?" the only words Jeeves recognises are *time* and *Bangkok*. It's good to know, but don't tell your students as it's great practice for them in forming correct questions using Wh- words, punctuation, etc.!

HANDS ON 🖰

You can ask Ask Jeeves all sorts of questions. Try some of these examples taken from the Ask Jeeves help pages, then try some of your own and see how accurate the results are:

- How many albums did Miles Davis make?
- How can I make chocolate cake?
- How tall is the Empire State Building?
- Where can I find photos of cats?
- Why is the sky blue?
- Who is the prime minister of Ghana?

You might be asking yourself why you should bother with the other ways of searching the Net when this seems to be so much easier. The simple answer to that is that there is no one single, complete database of all the pages on the Web – each search engine has different records, and there's a good chance that if you can't find it in one place, you'll find it in another. It really does help to use a selection.

It's also worth bearing in mind that a search engine is not always the quickest way to find things; some of the bigger sites such as Microsoft (http://www.microsoft.com), the BBC (http://www.bbc.co.uk) or the Encyclopedia Britannica (http://www.britannica.com) have enormous amounts of useful information.

TIP

Ask Jeeves has an excellent partner site called Ask Jeeves Kids. It only looks for pages and websites which are for kids and which are guaranteed to be free of 'adult' content. It's a great site to take younger learners for an introduction to the Internet.

Visit AJKids at http://www.ajkids.com

Making search choices

We've looked at three search engines here (and I went through a lot more of them while preparing this). No single Web search system includes all of the Internet in its databases. AltaVista and Yahoo! are often considered to be the best, but as we have seen here, they both have their good and bad points. It's a case of planning and experimenting until you find the right results. If you don't find what you're looking for with one of the three we've looked at here, have a look at this list of further search sites. But remember, as soon as you get to one of these pages, read the help file.

Excite   http://www.excite.com
Infoseek   http://www.infoseek.com
Lycos   http://www.lycos.com
Open Text   http://www.opentext.com
Webcrawler   http://webcrawler.com

1.5 Search FAQs

HOW DO I FIND IMAGES OR LINKS TO SPECIFIC PAGES AND SITES?

AltaVista features the possibility to search for a certain portion of a document (an image, a title, etc.). Try typing in *title:"The Electronic Telegraph"* to find pages with the phrase The Electronic Telegraph in the title. *link:its-online.com* matches pages that contain at least one link to a page with its-online.com in their address. Using *image:london.jpg* matches pages with london.jpg in an image tag, and *domain:br* finds pages from Brazil (.br is the country code for Brazil on the Internet).

WHY AREN'T MY SEARCHES WORKING WELL?

If you find you're getting no search results when you use AND and NOT, try using the mathematical symbols '+' and '-' instead. Depending on the search engine, these are used in place of the words. As I've already pointed out, the first thing you should do when you visit a search page is find out exactly how it works.

WHY AM I GETTING SO FEW RESULTS?

A recent survey of search engines found that they are fast falling behind in their efforts to catalogue the Internet, and that AltaVista – the biggest in terms of how many pages it has in its catalogue – is only aware of approximately 15% of the total content of the Internet. I always recommend starting with either AltaVista or Yahoo!, but it's worth bearing in mind that just because you don't find what you're looking for on one of these two pages, it doesn't mean that it isn't out there somewhere. Sometimes you'll have to use a selection of search pages before you find what you're looking for.

HOW DO I FIND TEACHING MATERIAL AND WEBSITES?

It's worth bearing in mind that if you are looking for something connected to teaching, another teacher will already have done the same thing, so a good way to find it is to use the network of listservs (see **Section 4**) and teaching websites (which follows) to help you out.

1.6 The Internet as resource bank

With these search techniques, and contact with other teachers through email, you should be getting pointers to great resources on a regular basis, and this should really be giving you some idea as to just how much useful material there is out there. Before we move on to the last part of this section in which we'll be looking at some considerations of using the Internet in class (as opposed to using material from the Net in class), here's a quick word about saving a little time when looking for foreign language resources in particular.

As teachers have been working with the Net for quite some time now, they have both developed their own sites full of useful material, and come across many others made by colleagues around the world. If you are looking for useful foreign language sites, it makes sense to see if anyone else knows where they are before setting off on a journey through AltaVista, Yahoo! and Ask Jeeves. With this in mind, here are three addresses where you will find a lot of links to language resources on the Net.

Dave's ESL Cafe – http://www.eslcafe.com
Apart from having plenty of useful sections itself, Dave's ESL Cafe has an enormous collection of links to EFL resources on the Web. It's a big site, so make sure you have a lot of spare time before digging under the surface.

its-online – http://its-online.com
its-online is a web-based magazine full of excellent lesson ideas, discussion pages and links to resources in many categories.

Net Language – http://www.net-language.com
Net Language has a large collection of pages devoted to language learning resources on the Internet. They are divided by language, and then into useful sections.

TIP ☑

There are plenty of links to these and other resources in the FAQs section. By the time you read this, some of them may have disappeared. For an updated list of useful links, check the website which accompanies this book at: http://www.cambridge.org/elt/chlt/internet

---

1.7 The Internet as a classroom tool

Any school which has a handful of computers can very easily and cheaply connect them to the Internet. Not only does this make it easier for teachers to gain access, but it also gives them the opportunity of introducing students to it as well. This opens up a world of possibilities as far as teaching goes, from giving students access to the 'world knowledge' they often don't have, putting them in touch with other students of the same language around the world, taking part in collaborative projects on a global scale, to sending their homework to their teacher by email.

But all this technology can also spell disaster in the wrong hands, or in the wrong circumstances. This section is a brief look at some of the considerations involved in using computers and the Internet in schools and some tips to follow for a smoother experience.

TIP ☑

If you teach a lot of business or in-company classes, there's a good chance that the companies where you work will have computers connected to the Internet. Use these to take advantage of some of the excellent corporate websites and business publications on the Net. (See the *FAQs* section at the back of the book.)

Before you take your students along to do any class based around the Web or email, you should be very sure that you know the technology yourself. Hopefully, if you have gone through *Section 1* so far, and have spent some time experimenting with the Net, you'll be feeling confident enough to introduce your students to it. Remember, apart from introducing your students to the Net, you may also be introducing them to basic computing skills as well. Before you start them on any kind of structured class, make sure they know how to start and shut down the computers, how to run a program, even how to move the mouse round the screen, point and click. However you do it – and you may find that you want to combine it with basic word processing skills – you must make sure that they are relaxed and unafraid to try things out (see *Section 2* for class plans dealing with first classes using computers and the Internet).

An Internet class needs to be as well-planned and structured as any other class. You must go through the material in advance and make sure that the language, content and presentation are what you want for your class. In addition to all these considerations, there are some other skills and points – perhaps not quite the normal language teacher preoccupations – which need to be taken into account.

Access to computers

It is rare for there to be one Internet-connected computer for every student in the class. As a general guide, one computer per three students works well for most Internet class activities, with each student taking a turn at 'driving'. For email penpal exchanges, one between two is better, and both students can be occupied at the same time by one dictating as the other types. Actually, it is often a bad idea to have one student per computer as this tends to discourage or inhibit conversation.

The archives of TESL-L (see *Section 4.1* for more information on TESL-L) have plenty of resources and records of past discussions dealing with ideal classroom layouts and classroom management techniques. Included in this part are two sample computer room layouts and considerations of their advantages and disadvantages.

Layout one has students working on a central table, with the teacher at the end equipped with a whiteboard and an overhead display of what they are doing, for students to follow. This has to be a reasonably big room with a table which allows for enough space between computers for books, dictionaries, etc. The biggest disadvantage to this layout is that students cannot readily see the people opposite them.

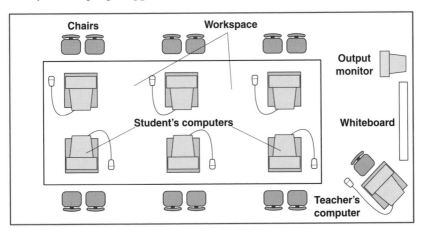

Layout one

Layout two has students working round the outside of the room, then swinging in on their chairs to work together with books, dictionaries, etc. and to get instruction from the teacher. While this layout provides a clear break between computer time and time spent on other activities (and stops people 'fiddling' when the teacher wants more control), it is difficult for every student to see the teacher at any given time.

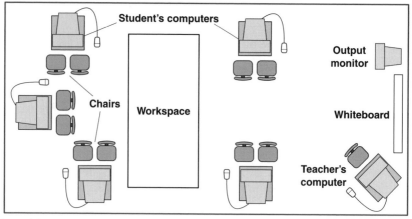

Layout two

Speed of access

As I pointed out at the beginning of this book, Internet access can be very slow at certain times of the day. It's important to know this, as it can help you prepare for your classes better. If, for instance, you are going to do a class which involves lots of multimedia elements such as video clips and sound files, it makes sense to download them in the morning, and save them on your hard disk. Later, when you need to use them, you won't have to rely on having a fast connection because they will be stored on your computer.

To save (rather than view online) a multimedia file such as a video or audio selection, click on it with your right mouse button and choose the *Save target as...* option, then choose a directory on your computer and click OK. Remember where you save it!

Page caching

Both Netscape and Explorer perform a function called caching. What this means is that when you visit a website, all the pages and images are automatically stored on your hard disk (you can see these files in the C:\Netscape\cache\ directory on your hard disk, if you are using Netscape or in the C:\Windows\Temporary Internet Files directory, if you are using Explorer). These pages are stored for a certain amount of time (specified in days), or until they reach a certain size (in megabytes). You can change these settings to suit your browsing habits (see **Section 4.4** for more information on how to set these).

When you go to a website, the first thing your browser does is see if it has the site saved in its cache – if it does, it displays it instantly. Then it goes and has a quick look at the original site to see if anything has changed – if that is the case, it updates the changed elements. If it can't find the site at all in its cache, it will perform its usual job of retrieving it from the Internet.

What this means to you is that if you visit the sites you want your students to visit just before the class starts, they will all be saved in the cache. When your students return to these sites a short while later, they will all come up much quicker than if they had to go and get them over the Net. Inevitably your students will want to branch out and visit sites you haven't stored in the cache, but even a little preparation helps.

Website life

There is little point planning an Internet class around a particular website unless you are sure that the site in question has a good pedigree and has been in existence for quite some time. While most professional websites are reliable and long-lasting, you may find the perfect site for a class, only to discover three days later that this site no longer exists. This usually only happens with personal homepages, but it has been known to happen with larger sites. The secret is to find two or three sites which deal with the same theme, leaving the lesson plan adaptable. Then if the site that you really want to use is not working, or has disappeared, you'll always have a back-up.

TIP ☑

Most personal homepages have this symbol ~ somewhere in their address: http://www.encomix.es/~dudeney/index.html

This symbol often doesn't appear on the keyboards of users outside the US. To make it, hold down the *Alt* key and type *126*. When you finally take your finger off the *Alt* key, the symbol will appear.

Technology breaks

And while we're on the subject of back-ups, it's worth bearing in mind that any class which revolves around technology needs a back-up plan for when the machinery breaks, or there's a power cut. There is very little you can do with a broken connection to the Net, or a set of websites which refuse to download. A little forewarning of your students will avoid a large part of the disappointment, should the situation arise.

Keeping control

There is no really simple solution to controlling access to programs in an open environment like a school. If you must do it you have to choose between password-protecting the whole system or using software which requires user identification before running a program. A quick look at these options will explain why they are generally more trouble than they are worth.

Start-up password

With this option, the computers cannot be turned on without someone typing in a password. This provides very good security, but also reduces the accessibility of the machines, making it necessary for the person who knows the password to be present every time they are turned on. As anyone who works with computers a lot will know, they often crash and stop working when you least expect them to, and if you have to keep asking for the password to be entered every time this happens you will quickly find this inconvenient.

Custom software

These mostly prohibit access to particular programs as defined by the person in charge, using combinations of usernames and passwords. They can be very effective as long as the password is not given to too many people. Again, though, people will share their passwords, forget them and find countless other ways of making this a troublesome procedure.

Having examined both of these options, I have to say that I am more in favour of relying on users' innate sense of responsibility, and on the assumption that there will always be a member of staff 'on duty' to control access to programs and Internet material.

This, coupled with a minimal installation of non-vital software (games, hardly-used applications, etc.) and an up-to-date anti-virus package usually proves sufficient. If you keep the programs installed on your computers to a minimum, and provide protection against viruses, you'll find your computer use should be as trouble-free as possible.

'Questionable' content

If you are using the Net with young or adolescent students, you should be aware that they could get access to some of this material and that it's your job to 'police' their activities while accessing information.

There are two ways to approach this problem:

The software approach

This software usually works in one of two ways:

1 Pages are checked for a certificate issued by a 'recognised' authority before they are displayed. These certificates indicate what kind of content the pages have, and the audience it is suitable for. If the pages have a certificate and the content is deemed suitable for the person browsing, the page will be displayed. If there is no certificate, the program blocks the site and a warning is issued.

2 Pages are checked for words in a database (these are generally connected with sex, violence, racial issues, etc). If any of them are found, the page is not displayed and a warning is issued. These databases generally come pre-configured with a set of words to which it is possible to add your own.

If you feel that you really do want to install software of this kind, you might like to take a look at the following products: SurfWatch; Net Nanny; CyberPatrol; CyberSitter.

They all do more or less the same job using one or both of the methods described above – but the results are never exactly what you would like, and can be more restrictive than really useful. With varied standards and different ways of 'grading' sites, it really is a hit-and-miss approach.

The conclusion has to be that censorship is a weighty matter, even when it does work, and with the plethora of standards currently under consideration, it becomes almost impossible to implement intelligently and with little fuss or negative impact on your teaching and your access to information. Common sense and a trust in people, along with good training and education should almost always ensure a fruitful and decent use of the facilities you make available to people.

The practical approach

There are a number of measures which you can take to ensure that your students are using the equipment as they are supposed to:

- make sure students realise that this is a facility which should be used, appreciated and not abused;
- make sure you're the only one to set passwords on anything;
- scan the hard drives regularly for .gif and .jpg images (the most common formats for images from webpages). If you suspect someone of downloading pornography or similar, check for new pictures after s/he has used the Internet;

- configure email programs to reject messages over a certain length, thus cutting down on the chance of someone having undesirable pictures and material sent to them by mail. Ask your technical staff or a friendly computer expert to help you with this;
- watch out for people giggling nervously over the other side of the room – it's a sure sign of something. Equally, notice whether the computer always suddenly crashes and needs to be re-started when you appear;
- check the Netscape Cache and Explorer Temporary Internet Files directories for suspect files (see *Page caching* covered earlier in this section);
- always have someone on hand to supervise Net access.

Most users won't even bother with the murkier side of the Net, but a firm warning of what is and what is not acceptable will do more good than an immediate ban.

2 Activities

This section introduces practical activities by theme and level. These activities take the teacher from the most basic introductory classes through a wide variety of popular themes (e.g. cinema, accommodation, the environment, news and media, etc.). Many of the activities have sample worksheets and are readily adaptable for most levels. Most of these activities were designed for use 'live', i.e. in a study centre equipped with computers connected to the Internet. If you are not in that position, you can still – with a little judicious printing, or some clever use of even one computer connected to the Net – use the great majority of them.

2.0 Activities by level

Some activities marked for students of Business English may not be explicitly designed for this purpose, but the themes and websites lend themselves to a simple adaptation for this field.

Young learners
2.1, 2.2, 2.5, 2.19, 2.25, 2.26, 2.29, 2.34, 2.37, 2.38, 2.41, 2.42, 2.47, 2.50, 2.55

Elementary
2.19, 2.23, 2.29, 2.34, 2.37, 2.38, 2.39, 2.42, 2.43, 2.47, 2.50, 2.55

Lower-intermediate
2.1, 2.2, 2.5, 2.8, 2.13, 2.15, 2.16, 2.18, 2.19, 2.23, 2.28, 2.34, 2.37, 2.39, 2.43, 2.50, 2.53, 2.55

Mid-intermediate
2.1, 2.2, 2.5, 2.8, 2.11, 2.12, 2.13, 2.15, 2.16, 2.18, 2.19, 2.21, 2.23, 2.27, 2.28, 2.31, 2.34, 2.35, 2.37, 2.39, 2.44, 2.49, 2.50, 2.52, 2.53, 2.55

Upper-intermediate
2.1, 2.2, 2.3, 2.4, 2.5, 2.7, 2.8, 2.9, 2.10, 2.11, 2.12, 2.13, 2.15, 2.16, 2.17, 2.18, 2.19, 2.20, 2.21, 2.22, 2.23, 2.24, 2.27, 2.28, 2.30, 2.31, 2.33, 2.34, 2.35, 2.36, 2.37, 2.44, 2.45, 2.46, 2.49, 2.50, 2.51, 2.52, 2.53, 2.54, 2.55

Advanced
2.1, 2.2, 2.3, 2.4, 2.5, 2.6, 2.7, 2.8, 2.9, 2.10, 2.11, 2.12, 2.13, 2.14, 2.15, 2.16, 2.17, 2.18, 2.19, 2.20, 2.21, 2.22, 2.23, 2.24, 2.27, 2.28, 2.30, 2.31, 2.32, 2.33, 2.34, 2.35, 2.36, 2.37, 2.40, 2.44, 2.45, 2.46, 2.48, 2.49, 2.50, 2.51, 2.52, 2.53, 2.54, 2.55

Business English
2.1, 2.2, 2.4, 2.6, 2.7, 2.10, 2.11, 2.16, 2.19, 2.21, 2.24, 2.28, 2.33, 2.35, 2.37, 2.49, 2.50, 2.54, 2.55

2.0.1 Activities by theme

This classification describes the principle theme of each activity

Advice: 2.3, 2.4

Animals: 2.43

Art: 2.36

Astrology: 2.22

Biography: 2.7

Books, reading: 2.17

Celebrations: 2.38

Cinema: 2.12, 2.31

Clothing: 2.34

Colours, shapes: 2.47

Computers, Internet: 2.1, 2.2, 2.26, 2.49, 2.55

Countries, nationalities: 2.29, 2.47

Describing people, things: 2.7, 2.22, 2.23, 2.24, 2.34

Entertainment: 2.44

Famous people: 2.6, 2.7, 2.8, 2.18, 2.36, 2.46

Food and drink: 2.25

Games, puzzles and quizzes: 2.37, 2.50

Holidays and travel: 2.14, 2.19, 2.20, 2.28, 2.30, 2.35, 2.38

House and home: 2.33, 2.48

Inventions: 2.54

Language: 2.15, 2.16

Logos: 2.21

Music: 2.5, 2.18

Mystery: 2.42, 2.45, 2.48

Names: 2.53

News: 2.10, 2.11, 2.41

Personality: 2.22, 2.23

Shopping: 2.32

Sport: 2.27

Survival: 2.51

Teenagers: 2.3, 2.52

Time: 2.29

Television: 2.13

World problems: 2.40

2.1 Introduction to the Net (I)

Summary: An introduction to basic Internet skills and concepts

Level: Lower intermediate and above

Time: 1 hour (30 minutes on the Net)

Language: Vocabulary connected with computers and the Internet

Sites: http://www.yahoo.com

Notes: This activity is designed to introduce students to the basic skills they will need for the other activities in this section.

Preparation

A simple questionnaire about computing habits is a good introduction to this activity. Make sure to include discussion questions about the Internet: has anyone used it? (at home / work / school?) What have they used it for? What can you find on the Net? Some questions are provided to help you. When they have finished talking, get feedback and general reactions to the subject. Then try the *Brief history of the Web* vocabulary activity.

Online

Show students how to open a web browser, type in an address and go to a website. Give students a printout of the Yahoo! main page. Go through the various functions of a browser (see *Section 1* for a reminder) and let students make notes and label their printout. Encourage them to play with Yahoo! and then to find a website connected with a hobby or interest (don't forget to show them how to *Bookmark* or add *Favorites*). When they find a page show them how to print it out. Make sure they know how to exit the browser and leave the computers tidy for the next class.

Offline

Put students into groups and give them time to compare their printouts and talk about the pages they have found. Discuss the process they have just been through and deal with the issues which usually arise – how long the page takes to appear, what information it provides.

Follow-ups / Variations

If you have good access to the Internet, give students more time in Yahoo!
They could prepare a presentation on an interest using pages they find.

Brief history of the Web

Read the terms and their meanings. Then fill in the gaps in the text.

Personal computers (PCs)	Small, computers which people use at work/home.
A network	Computers joined together so that they can communicate.
The Internet	A network of millions of computers around the world.
Email (Electronic mail)	A way of sending and receiving messages on the Internet.
The World Wide Web	A user-friendly way of looking at words, pictures and sounds on the Internet. Also called the Web or the WWW.
A browser	Computer software used to look at the Web.
A site	A place on the Internet, also called a webpage.
An address	The location of a site/webpage.

The .... has existed since 1969. It was created by
the USA military as a way of communicating even after a nuclear war.
Universities soon used it. At first it was only used to send and receive
.... messages. In 1969 computers were very big
and very expensive. Today millions of people use computers at home and
at work. Many people can afford to have a ....
at home and, at work, computers are joined over
...................................s. In 1991 what we know as the
.... was invented (Webpages themselves have
been around a lot longer). Now people looked at words, saw pictures and
even heard sounds from around the world on their PCs. The Web was
very popular. In 1987 there were 10,000 webpages but by 1992 there were
more than one million ....s and many millions
of webpages. Thirty years ago a few people used the Internet to send
email. Today, all you need is a PC and a .... like
Explorer to discover the wonderful world of the Web.

Computing habits

Have you got a computer at home? What do you use it for?
Do you use a computer at work / school / university? What for?
What do you know about the Internet?
Do you use it at home, at work? What do you use it for?
What can you find / have you found on the Net?
Do you have any 'keypals' (Internet penpals)?
Have you ever bought anything on the Net?

2.2 Introduction to the Net (II)

Summary: An introduction to searching the Internet

Level: Lower-intermediate and above

Time: 1 hour (50 minutes on the Net)

Language: Question forms

Sites: http://www.yahoo.com   http://www.altavista.com
http://www.askjeeves.com

Notes: Your students will often want to find specific information on the Internet. This activity teaches them how to search using different search pages. The *Trivia quiz* used to introduce the activity will need to be adapted to suit your group.

Preparation

Use a trivia quiz like the one which follows to generate interest. It's a good idea to include some questions they are certain to be able to answer without using the Net as well as some they probably won't.

Online

Introduce students to the different ways of searching using AltaVista, Yahoo! and Ask Jeeves (see *Section 1* for a reminder) and give them time to practise with the three sites. In groups, students try to finish the trivia quiz you've given them. When they have finished, give them some time to search for things they want to look at. The sample quiz below can be shortened to fit the time available, or you might like to try giving students a limited time to answer as many as possible, then pool results to see how the class as a whole has done.

Offline

In groups, students prepare a trivia quiz for their colleagues to do. This is a good opportunity to do some work on question forms. When the quizzes are ready, students can have a quick return visit to the Internet to practise their newly-acquired search skills.

Follow-ups / Variations

When the **Trivia quiz** has been done, students can prepare a similar quiz for you to try. In multinational groups, each country can be represented by a question for you to answer. This activity can easily be adapted for younger learners by substituting the search sites for Yahooligans! (http://www.yahooligans.com), Ask Jeeves Kids (http://www.ajkids.com) and Lycos Kids (http://www.lycos.com/kids/).

Trivia quiz – searching on the web

1 What's the name of the president of the United States?
2 Who invented the aspirin?
3 How many players are there in a basketball team?
4 What's the capital of Australia?
5 What's the weather like in Paris today?
6 How many albums have the Rolling Stones recorded?
7 What product is Jamaica famous for?
8 Which film won the Oscar for Best Picture in 1996?
9 Who was the first person in space?
10 Who wrote *One Hundred Years of Solitude*?

Use any of the search pages to find the answers you don't know.

© Cambridge University Press 2000

2.3 Giving advice

Summary: A look at teenage problems and giving advice

Level: Upper-intermediate and above

Time: 1 hour (20 minutes on the Net)

Language: Revision of functions for giving advice, reported
speech

Sites: http://www.teenadvice.org – archive section

Notes: This site features many problems dealing with sensitive
areas. Make sure you read through the problems you are
going to use thoroughly before looking at them in class.
You could also look at www.teentalk.com www.lucie.com
www.teenadvice.net

Preparation

In groups students talk about and list the kinds of problems they have
(or had) as teenagers. What advice were they given? What happened in the
end?

Divide the class into two groups and put the titles of some of the problems
from the Teen Advice Archive, which you looked up earlier, on the board.
(Make sure the problems are suitable and that the language used is what you
want to focus on in the class.) Each group should have about four titles. Give
them time to decide what they think the problems are about, who they think
is involved and what advice they would give the people.

Online

Introduce them to Teen Advice and give them time to find the problems you
gave them from the archive. They should go through the problems and see
if they guessed the content correctly. Ask them to make notes on the problems and advice given, writing down any language for giving advice that they
find.

Offline

Pair off students so that there is one person from each group, and get them to tell each other about the problems and advice they looked at. Ask them to compare the language for giving advice that they found. Write the examples on the board.

Follow-ups / Variations

There are plenty of good traditional activities for this kind of language work, including 'running counsellors' where half the class are counsellors and the other half have problems. (They don't have anything too sensitive.) Students with problems have a minute with each counsellor to explain their problem and get advice. At the end of the activity, votes are cast for the best counsellor.

Other options include a writing task where students are writing a case report on one of the problems, detailing the person and their problem, and the advice they were given – and making use of reported speech. Finally, why not try a class magazine (either on paper or as a web project – see *Section 3*) with a problem page?

2.4 I've always wondered ...

Summary: Finding out things you've always wanted to know

Level: Upper-intermediate and above

Time: 1 hour (30 minutes on the Net)

Language: Direct and indirect questions

Sites: http://www.askanexpert.com/askanexpert/

Notes: There are no guarantees that students will find answers to the questions they write. If this is the case, encourage them to use search engines to find the rest. See also http://www.ehow.com/

Preparation

Start the class with the *It's a mystery* activity provided. Give students time to think and complete the sentences, then get students to walk round asking questions to find someone who can answer the things they've written. When they've had time to get as much information as they can, discuss the possibility of finding the information on the Internet. Where would students look? (If they've done the search activities in *Activity 2.2 Introduction to the Net II* they should have a good idea.)

Online

Introduce students to the Ask an Expert site and give them time to look around for the people who might be able to help them. Some of the experts just have links to their websites where they say you should look first before contacting them personally by email; others have direct email links. If students can't find the answers to their questions, try the Ask Jeeves site. When they find answers to their questions, they should make notes. They may find this a fascinating site, so allow some time for exploration.

Offline

Students get into groups and swap interesting or unusual information they have found.

Follow-ups / Variations

A good follow-up is to do a class project on the town or city where you work e.g. you could call it 'Little-known facts about …' Another good follow-up activity is to walk around while students are using the Internet and make a note of the best, most interesting or most unusual questions to which students have been able to find an answer. If you work quickly you can make a 'Find someone who …' activity for later in the class (or the following lesson): take half a dozen of the things students have found an answer to and produce a quick questionnaire to distribute around the class. Students can then walk round the class asking questions until they find the answers, then noting the name of the person who supplied the information.

> **It's a mystery**
>
> Complete these sentences.
>
> 1 I'd love to know ....?
> 2 I've always wondered ....
> 3 I've no idea why ....
> 4 Why do you think ....?
> 5 Have you any idea ....?
> 6 Does anybody know ....?

2.5 A song class

Summary: Students prepare songs to present to the rest of the class

Level: Lower-intermediate and above

Time: 1 hour (40 minutes on the Net)

Language: Vocabulary connected with music

Sites: http://www.lyrics.ch http://www.yahoo.com

Notes: This class relies on you and your students being familiar with a word processor as well as the Internet. There is a sample song class on the website which accompanies this book at http://www.cambridge.org/elt/chlt/internet

Preparation

In pairs, use the **Talking music** discussion sheet to start the activity. Get some feedback and do a song activity of your own. These invariably lead to discussion between teacher and students as to what constitutes 'good' music.

Online

Introduce students to the International Lyrics Server site and show them how to search for lyrics. Ask the students (possibly in groups) to choose a song and to write the title of their chosen song on a piece of card. After they have read the lyrics on screen, ask them to draw a picture to illustrate the lyrics. Give each student a numbered piece of paper for the task.

Offline

The teacher collects all the pictures and titles, and displays them around the classroom. The students then have to match each numbered picture with the correct song title and discuss the reasons for their choice in the target language as they circulate, or alternatively write down the reasons for their choice.

Follow-ups / Variations

Ask students to chose three songs and to compare and contrast the words used. These could be either songs which are similar or completely different types.

Ask students to read the lyrics to a song of their choice (or at random) and to describe the mood, or summarise the story told or to write an extra verse in their own words.

Using Yahoo! students could also search the biographical information on their favourite music stars. These could then be turned into a presentation or project.

Talking music

In groups, discuss the following questions:

1 Who are your favourite music stars and groups?
2 What are your top five favourite albums of all time?
3 What is the best song ever recorded?
4 What's the best music video you've ever seen?
5 What's the best concert you've ever been to?
6 Do you prefer cassettes, mini discs, CDs or records?
7 Which groups or music stars do you dislike?
8 How much money do you spend on music each month?

Find out anything else you would like to know about your group's music habits.

© Cambridge University Press 2000

2.6 20th century news

Summary: Reviewing the 20th century

Level: Advanced

Time: 75 minutes (30 minutes on the Net)

Language: Past tenses, used to, descriptions

Sites: http://www.pathfinder.com/time/time100/index.html

Notes: This is the first of three activities looking at famous people. This first activity looks at famous people of the 20th century and examines their achievements. (See also *Activity 2.7 Heroes hall of fame* and *Activity 2.8 Celebrity dinner party*.)

Preparation

The Time site divides the people of the 20th century into five categories: leaders and revolutionaries (politics), artists and entertainers (the Arts), builders and Titans (business), scientists and thinkers (science), and heroes and icons (society). Put the five categories up on the board and brainstorm people to go in each category. Time has twenty in each section, so aim to get at least five from the class.

Online

Give students the opportunity to look at the names of people in the five categories. Who are they surprised by, and who is missing, in their opinion? Divide the class into two groups and get them to choose one person from each section, making sure they know a little about them and can explain why they think they should be chosen as the winner in their particular category.

Offline

Each group introduces their chosen winner in each category, giving a brief description of their life and achievements and saying why they should win. At the end of the presentations, the class votes for a winner for each section.

Follow-ups / Variations

There is a lot more to do at this site. Other features include the Time Warp section which compares 1900 to the end of the 20th century – useful for past tenses and structures such as 'used to' and 'didn't use to'. There is also a 20th century quiz (Test Your Knowledge) and other fun sections such as Event of the Century and 100 Worst Ideas. These could be used variously for comparisons, prediction exercises, etc.

2.7 Heroes hall of fame

Summary: A look at the heroes of modern life

Level: Upper-intermediate and above

Time: 90 minutes (40 minutes on the Net)

Language: Describing people, past tenses, present perfect

Sites: http://pathfinder.com/Life/heroes/hall.html

Notes: The 'heroes' found on this website are all real people, so fictional characters should not be included in the *Preparation* stage.

Preparation

Start this activity with a pyramid discussion. Individually, students make a list of their ten heroes (taken here to mean men and women) from both the past and present. Then in pairs, they discuss, compare and negotiate to make a list of ten from their twenty. Two pairs get together and repeat the process. The negotiations continue in bigger groups until the whole class has agreed on ten.

For a shorter activity, try brainstorming the names of heroes directly onto the board and having a class discussion on who the ten most important ones are, and why.

Online

Students visit the Life Hall of Heroes site and look at the list to see if any of their heroes appear. In groups students choose three heroes they don't know and have a look at their biographies, making notes. They then get into bigger groups to compare what they have found. Women are sadly missing from the Hall of Heroes – how did they do in the students' lists? The Distinguished Women of Past and Present site (http://www.netsrq.com/~dbois/) has the names of famous women divided up into categories (when searching choose *Field of Activity* option). Brainstorm famous women as a class activity then allow students to look around. Who did they forget?

Offline

Get feedback on what students have seen using the *Famous but forgotten?* activity below.

Follow-ups / Variations

In a single nationality class, you might like to look at how many people from that country figure in the Hall of Heroes. If there aren't any, brainstorm famous people from the country. In mixed nationality classes, the same can be done, with students telling the rest of the class who their national heroes are.

Other possible follow-ups include a visit to http://www.biography.com for some games and puzzles in the famous person quiz or anagram game. Another good site for general information on famous people is the Famous Birthdays site at http://oeonline.com/~edog/bday.html where students can see who shares a birthday with them. This is also a good opportunity for students to do a written assignment on a famous person from their country. For help in writing a biography, they could have a look at the Biography Maker – a guide to how to write a good biography – at http://www.bham.wednet.edu/bio/biomak2.htm This also makes an ideal topic for an extended project or website (see *Section 3* for details).

Famous but forgotten?

What did you think of the Hall of Heroes site – were you surprised by the content?

Who do think was there, but shouldn't have been?

Who do you think should have been there, but wasn't?

Who are the heroes from your country?

What do you think the criteria should be for being famous?

If you could be famous, what would you like to be famous for?

2.8 Celebrity dinner party

Summary: Finding out about famous people

Level: Lower-intermediate and above

Time: 60 minutes (30 minutes on the Net)

Language: Past tenses, ordering and prioritising, supporting decisions and giving reasons

Sites: http://www.celebsites.com http://www.yahoo.com

Notes: Current celebrities can be found at the CelebSites website. For older famous people, dead ones or the scientist / politician / writer range, use Yahoo! sections. This can also be adapted for business English classes, using appropriate figures from the world of business, finance, etc.

Preparation

For this activity you'll need some pictures of famous men and women (living or dead). Try to find a selection of scientists, politicians, pop stars, actors, writers, etc. Display the pictures and elicit any information the class knows about the people. If you lack the time or resources to prepare an activity like this, simply provide the names of celebrities, or perhaps have a quick quiz, with you providing surnames and the class providing the first names as you write them on the board.

Explain that for this activity they should imagine that the class has won a competition to host a celebrity dinner party and that they can invite four of the people shown.

Online

Use the sites listed or give students a chance to practise their search skills. In pairs, they have thirty minutes to find out about the people they are not familiar with, and make some notes on their achievements and reasons for being famous. When they have finished, they should be in a position to decide who to invite.

Offline

Give everyone a seating plan and give each pair a chance to arrange their guests around the table in such a way that everyone will have somebody interesting to talk to. Then put pairs together to discuss their arrangements. They should explain:

who they have invited and why;
why they have people sitting next to each other;
where they themselves would sit;
what they would like to ask their guests.

Follow-ups / Variations

There are plenty of opportunities to adapt and extend this activity. Students might like to plan the menu for the evening (are any of the celebrity guests vegetarian?), or perhaps arrange an interview with their favourite guest. The interview can then be written up.

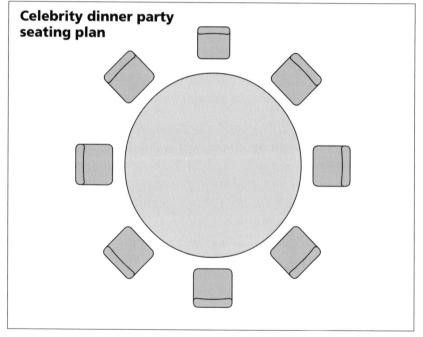

Celebrity dinner party seating plan

© Cambridge University Press 2000

2.9 The weather

Summary: Talking about weather and extreme weather conditions

Level: Upper-intermediate and above

Time: 60 minutes (30 minutes on the Net)

Language: Weather vocabulary, describing the weather, numbers, facts and figures

Sites: http://www.weather.com/breaking_weather/encyclopedia/index.html#bol

Notes: Standard weather information can be obtained at http://weather.yahoo.com

Preparation

Start with some work on the various ways of talking about the weather (it's sunny, the sun is shining, etc.). Brainstorm vocabulary to complete the grid below. With lower level classes, you might like to provide them with the vocabulary they need to complete the grid and have students classify it according to the headings:

Destructive	Serious	Noteworthy	Normal
tornado	....	boiling	warm
....	....	....	....
....	....	....	....
....	....	....	....

© Cambridge University Press 2000

Online

Divide students into As and Bs and give them either five mythical people (Zeus, Thor, Jupiter, Indra and Helios) or five historical figures (Cleveland Abbe, Anders Celsius, Gustave Coriolis, Daniel Fahrenheit and Evangelista Torricelli). They then visit the Weather Channel's Storm Encyclopaedia and find out as much as they can about the people they have been given, and what their connection is to the weather. As and Bs then get together to discuss what they have found out. The Storm Encyclopaedia has plenty of different sections for different types of weather. Give students a chance to visit these (flooding, heatwave, etc.) to complete the vocabulary grid they started in the preparation section.

Offline

Get feedback on the information about the people and correct the vocabulary grid.

Follow-ups / Variations

This lends itself nicely to a typical newspaper disaster headline and story, if you can find some pictures of tornadoes, floods, etc. Pass round the pictures and put some headlines like the following up on the board: *Floods leave French Farmers Fuming / Canadian Catastrophe Catches Careless Campers Catnapping / Twister Tears Town Apart.* Have a close look at the headlines and brainstorm some possible facts and events related with each one before leaving the students to write the final article.

Another fun activity is to use webcams – cameras connected to the Net – to find out what the weather is like at the moment. Visit http://www.windows2000.com/cams1.htm for details.

2.10 Strange news

Summary:	A short activity based around news headlines from Yahoo! / Reuters
Level:	Upper-intermediate and above
Time:	1 hour (20 minutes on the Net)
Language:	Telling stories, anecdotes, conversational skills
Sites:	http://www.yahoo.com/headlines
Notes:	The stories at the Yahoo! headlines site change regularly, so it is not a good idea to choose your headlines too far in advance. This activity is an ideal one for doing entirely offline if necessary. The Yahoo! news site also features business news. I have found this to be an excellent quick activity for higher level students.

Preparation

Get some topical cartoons or news headlines from newspapers and magazines and pass them out in groups. Students try to remember (or guess) what the stories were. Can they remember anything curious or funny which has happened recently?

Divide the class into groups and give each group three or four headlines from the curious stories section of Yahoo! News Headlines. Can they guess what the stories are? They make predictions as to what they think each story could be about. You can also do a vocabulary prediction exercise – which words would they expect to find in each article?

Online

Students visit the Yahoo! News Headlines site and find their stories. They then read them and make notes.

Offline

Later students get into bigger groups – or as a whole class activity – and tell each other their stories, including new (and useful) words they have learnt.

Follow-ups / Variations

You could take a look at some language used for swapping anecdotes: 'This is a great one ...', 'This one's funny ...', 'I've never heard that one before ...', etc. There are also plenty of Urban Myth sites on the Net (a quick search of Yahoo! or AltaVista will turn up quite a few) which can easily be exploited in this context.

A writing activity where students write the article, based on strange headlines you provide is also a good follow-up.

2.11 Making the news

Summary: Designing the perfect newspaper

Level: Intermediate and above

Time: 60 minutes (30 minutes on the Net)

Language: Vocabulary connected with the news

Sites: http://www.crayon.net

Notes: This can also be used with business English classes as a good warmer, with students dipping into their newspaper before, or at the start of class.

Preparation

You could start with the *In the news* activity, getting feedback and general opinions on what is and what isn't considered interesting to your students. Alternatively, brainstorm some vocabulary connected with newspapers (e.g. broadsheet, tabloid, headline, article) and their different sections.

Put students into groups and get them to design the perfect newspaper – they should discuss the following criteria and agree on final details. They should think about:

The title of the newspaper;
The newspaper's motto (e.g. Tomorrow's News Today!);
The sections it would have, and their order.

Online

The Crayon website allows people to create their own newspapers, complete with title, motto and sections. The news which then fills this paper is taken from free Internet news sources. Students fill in a form at the website and submit their newspaper. They are then given a unique web address where they can consult their newspaper. Crayon automatically updates the different sections on a daily basis, so once the newspaper has been designed it will always be up-to-date.

Offline

Students can compare and talk with other groups about the newspapers they have designed. This can then lead on to a discussion about the quality and content of newspapers available locally.

Follow-ups / Variations

Introduce the idea of a class or school magazine or newspaper which can either be done in the traditional way or as a website (see *Section 3*). Or bring in examples of real newspapers in the language you are teaching and allow students to have a look through them.

In the News

In groups, talk about your preferences and reading habits.

- What newspapers and magazines do you read?
- Do you read a newspaper every day? And on Sunday?
- What are your favourite sections of a newspaper?
- What sections do you never read?
- Do you read your horoscope every day?
- Do you read the cartoons?
- What would your ideal newspaper have in it?

© Cambridge University Press 2000

2.12 Film reviews

Summary: Writing and publishing film reviews

Level: Mid-intermediate and above

Time: 90 minutes (30 minutes on the Net)

Language: Vocabulary connected with movies and the cinema

Sites: http://www.imdb.com

Notes: The Internet Movie Database is the biggest movie resource on the Net. There is no guarantee that film reviews submitted to the Internet Movie Database will actually ever appear on the site. If this is likely to cause disappointment you might like to consider turning this into your own website (see *Section 3*).

Preparation

Use the film reviews sheet to start off the activity. Get feedback and then brainstorm vocabulary connected with films (types, people involved, etc.). Working in pairs, get students to write the name of a favourite film on a piece of paper and give it to their partner – the partner then has to get as much information as possible by asking relevant questions. Each partner should make notes about the film as they are talking.

Online

Visit the Internet Movie Database and give students time to look at the reviews section, noting how each review can have lots of different parts. You might want to prepare a quiz along the lines of: *Who was the leading actress in Titanic?* etc.

Offline

When students have a good feel for the personal reviews which are submitted to the site they can start to plan theirs. Get them to look back over the notes which were made for them in the preparation stage and begin to flesh them out until they have a complete film review. Correct and encourage re-writes and peer critique until the reviews are good enough to submit to the site.

Follow-ups / Variations

This would be a good opportunity to do a video session with a film, video or part of a film with your class. You can find useful back-up and preparatory material at Hollywood Com (http://www.hollywood.com). Another useful site for preparing film sessions in class is Drew's Script-o-Rama http://www.script-o-rama.com which features film scripts for over 300 major feature films.

Film reviews

Think about your views on the cinema, then talk to a partner.

• What sort of films do you like?
• When was the last time you went to the cinema?
• Who are your favourite actors and actresses?
• Do you prefer the cinema or watching videos?
• What are the best and worst films you have ever seen?

© Cambridge University Press 2000

2.13 Square eyes

Summary: Talking about television / Deciding what to watch

Level: Lower-intermediate and above

Time: 75 minutes (30 minutes on the Net)

Language: Television vocabulary, agreeing and disagreeing, giving opinions

Sites: www.bbc.co.uk www.centraltv.co.uk www.channel4.co.uk – listings section

Notes: Can be done offline with printed material from the Internet. This idea can be done with TV listings from any country which has a selection of channels. Although this activity uses British TV pages, it is easily adapted for most countries since many TV companies now have online schedules.

Preparation

Hand out copies of a local newspaper's TV page. Ask students to go through the listings and make a note in English of the different types of TV programmes they can find (e.g. documentary, soap opera). Feed in vocabulary as necessary, then get feedback as a group. Give out the ***Viewing habits*** questionnaire and, working in pairs, students talk about and compare their views on TV.

Online

Tell students they are going to have a quiet night at home and that they need to find something to watch from 6 pm to 10 pm, for example. Give them time to look at the different websites and choose their programmes. They should make notes of times, descriptions and channels.

Offline

In pairs or small groups, students negotiate and agree on a viewing schedule. With lower level groups you may need to do some pre-teaching of structures used for agreeing / disagreeing and giving opinions. When they have agreed on what they are going to watch, combine two groups and repeat the process until the whole class has agreed on what to watch that night.

Follow-ups / Variations

Individually, students watch a programme and write a short review. With higher levels, English language newspapers usually have good TV review pages which can be used for exemplification or as a starting point.

This is also an ideal opportunity to do some work on the 'opinion' style of writing task where students are asked to state the case for a particular issue such as debating the statement '*TV is nothing but sex, violence and repeats*'.

Viewing habits

1 How many hours a day do you spend watching TV?
2 What type of programmes do you watch?
3 What type of programmes do you never watch?
4 What's your favourite programme?
5 Do you watch a soap opera? Which one?
6 What did you watch last night?
7 Do you watch 'serious' programmes like the news, documentaries, etc.?
8 Do you watch the adverts?
9 Do you ever video any programmes?
10 Which programmes would make you want to watch TV all evening?

2.14 Eco-tourism

Summary: Planning and reporting on exotic holidays with an ecological slant

Level: Advanced

Time: 90 minutes (45 minutes on the Net)

Language: Past and future tenses, holiday vocabulary, experiences

Sites: http://www.greentravel.com

Preparation

Use the *Holidays – past and future* activity to start the class. Get feedback on the discussion and introduce the idea of eco-tourism and find out if anyone has ever had a holiday which focussed on that. Ask students to think of parts of the world where this might take place. Brainstorm vocabulary on activities, places to stay and the kind of thing you would have to take with you on such a holiday.

Online

Students visit the Green Travel Network site and do the What Kind of Traveller Are You? quiz. Choose the Trip Ideas page and give each student a different destination. Each destination has maps, activities, where to go, trip options, costs and a travellers talk section. Get them to work through their holiday, making notes. Then as a whole class compare and discuss, and decide on a final location to go on holiday.

Offline

Students now create a tour of their country for adventurous travellers advising them on where they should go, what they should see and do on the holiday. In mixed nationality classes, students could bring photos and information from their countries to do a presentation in a follow-up class.

Follow-ups / Variations

Divide the class into groups of potential travellers and travel agents. Travel agents prepare by looking at the holiday descriptions while travellers prepare a set of questions they want to ask about possible holidays.

The Green Travel Network pages also include Travel trivia quizzes and a Travellers talk section for travel anecdotes. This is a good opportunity to work on story-telling techniques, and an ideal opportunity to introduce a writing activity.

Holidays – past and future

In groups, talk about your holiday experiences and wishes.

- What's the best holiday you've ever had?
- What's the worst holiday you've ever had?
- Who do you like going on holiday with?
- Do you prefer an active or a lazy holiday?
- What do you pack when you go on holiday?
- Which countries have you visited and which would you like to visit?
- If you were very rich, what would you do on holiday?
- Where would you never go on holiday?

© Cambridge University Press 2000

2.15 A little *Je ne sais quoi*

Summary: Borrowed words in English

Level: Lower-intermediate and above

Time: 45 minutes (15 minutes on the Net)

Language: Foreign words and expressions used in everyday English

Sites: www.ultisoft.demon.co.uk/borrow.html

Notes: Can be done offline with printed material from the Internet. This webpage has a lot of information, so be careful to focus students on the task.

Preparation

Hand out copies of the **Borrowed words** quiz and give students a little time to match the words and countries. Get some feedback on their decisions, but don't go over the correct answers yet.

Online

Get students to go to the Borrowed words website and find the words from the quiz, noting where the words came from. Quick finishers can have a look round this page and find out if there are any words in English which have been borrowed from their own language.

   This is an ideal opportunity to teach students how to search for something on a webpage – click *Edit*, then choose *Find (on this page)* and enter the word you're searching for, followed by a click on the *Find Next* button. This will cut down significantly the quantity of reading involved.

Offline

Get feedback on the correct answers. Now brainstorm the activity in reverse, with students thinking of a list of English words which are used in their own language. Do equivalents exist in the original language? The world of technology is particularly rife with English words.

Follow-ups / Variations

With higher level groups, a discussion about 'language purity' works very well, with students tackling issues such as the evolution of language, 'inventing' new words, etc. With lower level groups, a map of the world can be used to practise country names and languages, with countries also being illustrated with a word which English has borrowed.

Borrowed words

Match the words used in English on the left with the language they came from originally.

1. ketchup	A. Inuit
2. robot	B. Japanese

3. paper	C. Italian
4. igloo	D. Cantonese
5. biscuit	E. Turkish
6. kindergarten	F. Czech
7. graffiti	G. French
8. karate	H. Spanish
9. yoghurt	I. Ancient Egyptian
10. siesta	J. German

© Cambridge University Press 2000

KEY: ketchup – Cantonese / robot – Czech / paper – Ancient Egyptian / igloo – Inuit / biscuit – French / kindergarten – German / graffiti – Italian / karate – Japanese / yoghurt – Turkish / siesta – Spanish

2.16 The same language?

Summary: US and UK English

Level: Lower-intermediate and above

Time: 1 hour (30 minutes on the Net)

Language: American and British English variants

Sites: http://pages.prodigy.com/NY/NYC/britspk/ukus1.html

Notes: This is one of many sites dealing with the difference between American and British English, and one of the better ones since it doesn't 'take sides'. Be sure to check the http://pages.prodigy.com/NY/NYC/britspk/dictlink.html page which has links to other resources in this area

Preparation

Take ten American English words which are different in British English. Easy words include: drug store (chemist), gasoline (petrol), pants (trousers), cab (taxi), elevator (lift), store (shop), cop (policeman/policewoman), fries (chips), sidewalk (pavement) and trunk (boot). Put them into sentences to add some context, e.g. *Your room is on the seventh floor, Sir. You have to take the elevator* or *Please join the line to buy tickets for the next show.* Students work in pairs to decide what the British English equivalents are.

Online

This website has two-way conversion (e.g. British to American and American to British English) and each section is divided up into four pages, alphabetically. Give students time to find out if they have the right conversions. Now hand out the **What did you say?** activity which they convert to British English. Get feedback and correct where necessary.

Follow-ups / Variations

This activity works both ways, so if you teach predominantly American English, you can change the focus of the tasks easily. It can open up into an extended discussion on the differences in English around the world, and whether British English or American English is predominant in the countries where the students come from. For lower levels, try replacing the **What did you say?** activity with a set of pictures representing the different things.

What did you say?

James is on holiday in the United States. He's from London and is having problems with some of the vocabulary. Can you help him do the shopping?

'Well James, it's good to have you here in New York finally. Can you run out to the store and get some food, I haven't had time? OK, here's what we need ...

... a few packets of potato chips for the party. You'll have to go to the liquor store, too, and get some beer. Then we also need some cheese, crackers and relish. We don't want everyone to be hungry.

OK, then we need to eat tomorrow. Can you get some ground beef – we can have that with fries or baked potatoes. Get some granola and dried fruit – golden raisins, that kind of thing – you need to go to the health food store for those. Oh, and get some bread and jelly for breakfast. I think that's everything – thanks a lot.'

© Cambridge University Press 2000

2.17 A good book

Summary: Talking about reading habits

Level: Upper-intermediate and above

Time: 90 minutes (20 minutes on the Net)

Language: Vocabulary connected with books and reading

Sites: http://www.amazon.com

Notes: There are now plenty of online bookshops, although Amazon continues to have the biggest stock. The best section is the Best Sellers – Paperback Fiction page with information on current popular books.

Preparation

Start brainstorming vocabulary on books, reading and reading habits. Pre-teach any of the words from the *Are you a bookworm?* activity which you think might cause problems. In pairs, students do the activity. Get them to take notes as they'll need that information again. Get feedback as a class and discuss general reading habits.

Online

The Amazon Com Best Sellers Paperback Fiction section has news and reviews of current paperback bestsellers. There are short reviews of the top-selling novels of the moment and reviews from members of the public. Each student has to find a novel for the person they talked to during the preparation stage, and one for themselves. They should then get back into their original pairs and explain what they have chosen and why.

Offline

Prepare some colour photocopies of book covers for students to look at, but try to remove any blurb or information about the books themselves. If you can't prepare these yourself, use a selection of books from home or the library, but limit access to the front cover only.

Go over the different parts of a standard book blurb, taking a real book as an example, or perhaps using one from the Amazon site. This usually includes a short summary of the story, reviews from newspapers, comments about the author, etc. Students have to look at the covers of the books, select one that inspires them and create the blurb, including some or all of the parts.

Follow-ups / Variations

For very high levels, the 'first line' game can be fun. Take a selection of books and give one to each student. In turn, each student reads out their blurb and then copies out the first line of the book onto a strip of paper. Everyone else then writes what they think the first line might be on separate strips of paper. When everyone has finished, the student collects all the first lines (including his or her original one) and reads them out. Students get five points for guessing the correct first line (i.e. the original), and they also win ten points from each student who guessed that they wrote the real one.

Are you a bookworm?

Ask your partner these questions:

- Not including textbooks, how many books do you buy a month?
- How do you choose a book: by the cover, the blurb, the name of the author or something else?
- What is your favourite type of novel?
- Where do you usually read: in bed, on the train, in the bath …?
- Do you have a favourite literary character or hero?
- Do you ever use a library, or do you prefer to buy books?
- Do you have a favourite author whose books you always read?
- Do you prefer to see the film first and then read the novel or vice versa?
- What was the title of the last novel you read? Who was the author?

2.18 Ladies and gentlemen ... The Beatles

Summary: Famous Beatle songs

Level: Lower-intermediate and above

Time: 1 hour (30 minutes on the Net)

Language: Talking about famous people, biographies

Sites: http://www.yahoo.com – Music-Artists-Beatles section

Notes: More 'scholarly' information can be found at http://www.getback.org which includes a 'Today in Beatles History' section.

Preparation

Students complete the *Mind the gap* activity. They may not be able to finish it. Brainstorm information about The Beatles. What does the class know about the group, and what would they like to know? Make a collaborative list of things to find.

Online

There are a lot of Beatles sites in the Yahoo! section, so give students time to go through them and find the information they need. It would be a good idea to focus on the Yahoo! website summaries for categories, teaching students to look for relevant words such as 'discography' for the song titles and 'biography' for general group information. Students should check their answers to the *Mind the gap* activity and find the information they wanted to know.

Offline

Get feedback on the song titles and make sure the class has found the information needed. The information collected can then be built up into a small biography of The Beatles, or a Twenty Things You Didn't Know About The Beatles article.

Follow-ups / Variations

Personalise the activity with more Internet time for students to find out a bit more about their favourite groups for a future writing project, including discography, biography, pictures, etc. For lower levels, this is an ideal opportunity for the celebrity interview practising the present tense, adverbs of frequency, etc. with students taking turns to play the part of a celebrity.

Mind the gap

These are all Beatles song titles. Can you complete them?

1 Lucy in the Sky with ....
2 Strawberry Fields ....
3 Can't Buy me ....
4 Do You Want to Know a ....
5 .... Days a Week
6 Hello ....
7 Yellow ....
8 ....
9 She's .... Home
10 Hard Day's ....

© Cambridge University Press 2000

2.19 Mystery postcards

Summary: Describing places, food, people, etc.

Level: Elementary and above

Time: 1 hour (30 minutes on the Net)

Language: Past tenses, present perfect, adjectives

Sites: http://www.all-yours.net/program/start20?write938159&lan=en

Notes: If this site is not to your liking, try a search for something like "virtual postcard" in Yahoo! or AltaVista for a selection of similar websites. You'll need email addresses for your students (see the *FAQs* section).

Preparation

Hand out a copy of the **Mystery postcard** and ask students where they think Graham and Cindy are on holiday. The answer is Paris, France. The clues are Tower, boat on the river, art gallery, croissants, wine, Disney. Now ask them to think of somewhere they would like to go on holiday and to make a list of the things they would do and see there. This can also be done with somewhere they have already been.

Online

Divide students into pairs. Go to the Digital Internet Postcard site (listed above) and give students time to prepare and send a mystery postcard to their partner. This involves choosing an image, writing the text for the card and addressing it (email address), previewing it to make sure it looks fine and then clicking the send button.

Note: When a postcard is sent, notification is sent via email to the recipient who then has to return to the site to 'collect' the card. This is usually very quick, but you may need to continue this activity in a subsequent class if the cards don't arrive quickly enough. When the students have picked up their postcards, print them out.

Offline

Display the postcards in the classroom and give students time to walk around deciding where everyone is on holiday. They should make notes of the clues which helped them work out the answers. Get feedback and check everyone is right.

Follow-ups / Variations

For higher levels, work on country stereotypes can be done, concentrating on adjectives and concepts used to describe people from different countries (e.g. English people all wear bowler hats, carry an umbrella and a copy of *The Times*. They are cold and a little arrogant ...). What is the purpose of stereotypes, and how much truth is there in them? For lower levels, a holiday diary is a fun follow-up.

Mystery postcard

Dear Mum and Dad,

It's really great here! The flight wasn't very long and we had good food on the plane. It's a very expensive city, so we haven't been out too much. You were right, the view from the top of the Tower is amazing, you can see all of the city. Today we're going on a boat on the river and then to visit a couple of old churches before we go to that art gallery you told us about. We've had lots of croissants and coffee for breakfast – very cheap! The wine is also good and cheap. Disney at the weekend!

Love, Graham and Cindy

Mr and Mrs Thomas

3 Blackberry Way

Gloucester

GR1 4XY

England

2.20 A terrible holiday

Summary: Talking about holidays – good and bad

Level: Upper-intermediate and above

Time: 1 hour (30 minutes on the Net)

Language: Past tenses, travel vocabulary

Sites: http://www.independent.co.uk/travel/index.html

Notes: *The Independent* newspaper's travel section is full of useful information for travellers. Here we look at the regular 'Your Holiday Disaster' page and the 'Your Questions, Our Experts' feature.

Preparation

Brainstorm travel vocabulary in the following categories: getting there (transport and travelling), things to take (what to pack), where to stay (types of holiday accommodation), what to do (holiday activities), people (hotel staff, tour guides, other tourists, etc.). Build up a comprehensive list of vocabulary for students to use later. Hand out the ***Best and worst*** questionnaire and give students time to think and make notes before pairing them off to compare and discuss.

Online

As the 'Your Disaster Holiday' section of the website is regularly updated, you'll need to look at it shortly before the class to make sure what you expect to be there is actually there. Either prepare specific comprehension questions, or just get students to identify who is writing, what kind of holiday they were expecting, what went wrong and how the story ended. You might also initiate a discussion on which holiday was the most disastrous.

Offline

Using the structure and ideas from the website, students can now write up their disaster holiday.

Follow-ups / Variations

The disaster holiday articles could be displayed for review and comment. Students could also play the part of a travel company representative writing a letter of apology or explanation for the terrible holidays. Using the 'Your Questions, Our Experts' feature as a starting point, build up a list of tips and advice for people visiting the countries of your students.

Best and worst

Think about all the holidays you've had. Which one was the best, and which the worst? Make notes in the space below ...

BEST   WORST

Reason.................................... Reason..

Where..................................... Where..

© Cambridge University Press 2000

Who with	Who with ....
Weather	Weather ....
Food	Food ....
Company	Company ....
Activities	Activities ....

2.21 A new logo

Summary: Talking about logos, company philosophy and image

Level: Mid-intermediate and above

Time: 1 hour (20 minutes on the Net)

Language: Descriptions, making predictions

Sites: http://casciodesign.com/n-multi.html

Preparation

Students bring examples of their company (or school) logo, letterheads and any other material which identifies the corporate image of the place where they work or study. They introduce their company/school and show how the features, services and philosophy of the company is reflected in the materials.

Online

This page at Cascio Design has over thirty logos created for different companies by the design studio. Encourage students to look at the logos and predict what kind of company might have a logo like that. They should talk in groups and make predictions. Then allow them time to look at the descriptions of the logos which interest them by clicking on the logo and going to the corresponding page.

Offline

Bearing in mind what they have just seen, ask them to cast a more critical eye over their company/school image and discuss in groups what they think they might be able to do with it. If there are any artists (amateur or professional) in the class, ask them to help with the new designs.

Follow-ups / Variations

Students could prepare a report for a design company, summarising their company/school image, philosophy and services and asking for a re-design of their logo, stationery, etc.

2.22 Written in the stars

Summary: Talking about character / horoscopes

Level: Upper-intermediate and above

Time: 90 minutes (30 minutes on the Net)

Language: Character adjectives, making predictions

Sites: http://www.astrology-online.com – horoscope section

Notes: There are two sections to this site, the first gives general information about star signs, the second gives a weekly horoscope (updated on Saturdays).

Preparation

Do the *What are they like?* activity to do some basic work on the kind of character adjectives which usually occur in horoscopes. Does the class believe in them? Do students read their horoscope every day? What star sign are the students – and do they fit into the general description for that sign?

Online

Give half the class six star signs, and the other half the remaining six. Give them time to visit the website and make some notes on the descriptions given to each sign. At the top of each page there is a quick summary for the sign, so they don't have to go through the long descriptions which follow.

Offline

You should now have an information gap activity with students being able to get together in pairs and ask and answer questions about the signs they didn't investigate. They can then chat about their personal horoscopes for the week. Do they think anything will come true (or has anything already come true?).

Follow-ups / Variations

A 'Find someone who . . .' activity can work well here. Higher levels can have a more in-depth discussion about prediction, astrology, etc.

You could also let them visit the page with their horoscope for the week and make some notes on what they can expect and compare the predictions in small groups. You can follow up on this in a later class: did any of it come true?

What are they like?

How would you describe someone who ...

gives away lots of money?	generous
never buys you a drink?	....
easily loses their temper?	....
never loses their temper?	....
helps other people?	....
only thinks about themselves?	....
jokes about everything?	....
never jokes about anything?	....
expects good things to happen?	....
expects bad things to happen?	....
believes whatever you tell them?	....
doubts what you tell them?	....
worries about what people think?	....
doesn't care what people think?	....
likes going to parties?	....
doesn't like going to parties?	....
lets people down?	....
never lets people down?	....
has a high opinion of themself?	....
doesn't boast?	....

© Cambridge University Press 2000

2.23 People watching

Summary: Describing people

Level: Elementary and above

Time: 1 hour (20 minutes on the Net)

Language: Adjectives, activities, present continuous

Sites: http://www.onlinephotogallery.com/peopleof.htm

Notes: Also try searching for 'pictures of people' on AltaVista. There are a lot of image archives on the Net. These usually contain copyright material, so you can look at them on screen, but there are usually rules about saving them onto your own computer. Check before you do.

Preparation

This activity requires some pre-online work on descriptions: physical characteristics, clothing, location and activity. I have often used the Suzanne Vega song 'Tom's Diner' as a scene-setting device since it features descriptions of people in a café and is easily exploitable for the present continuous. The song itself can be done as a gap-fill with the participles removed, and students can be invited to imagine or even illustrate the scene they hear in the song (remember, you can find the lyrics on the Net – see *Activity 2.5 A song class*).

Online

The gallery of photos in the website is a selection of thumbnail images (small versions of larger ones) which can be clicked and enlarged. Give students time to look around and decide on one photo they find particularly interesting. They should then imagine: who the person is, where they live and what they are like, what they do (job and hobbies) and what their life is like. They should rough out a quick description of the person. These can be stuck to the wall, and the class can read them and try to identify the person on screen.

Offline

With the details they have got from the photo, and their notes, a longer description can now be worked on, with students extending the short notes they made in the online part of the activity to a detailed description of the person and their life.

Follow-ups / Variations

Very low levels can use this activity on one particular basis, concentrating simply on clothes, or physical description, or activity.

With more creative classes, try incorporating the characters chosen and described into a song (following the example of Tom's Diner), or a simple poem.

With higher levels, some useful work can be done on stereotyping. What assumptions underlay their guesses, and were they fair assumptions? (e.g. a fair assumption might be that a blond-haired person is likely to be from Northern Europe, whereas an ungrounded prejudice might be that someone with glasses is probably an intellectual, etc.).

2.24 Get a job

Summary: Finding the right job / talking about skills and character

Level: Upper-intermediate and above

Time: 1 hour (30 minutes on the Net)

Language: Personality adjectives, occupations, describing daily routine

Sites: http://www.ncsu.edu/careerkey/

Notes: The personality quiz can be done online, or downloaded and printed. If students already know what kind of personality they have, they can go straight to the Jobs That Fit My Personality section.

Preparation

Use a copy of a jobs page from an English language newspaper for an intro-ductory speed reading activity with general comprehension questions such as, which company wants dynamic young managers? Or, where will you get two months' paid holiday per year. (If you don't have access to a newspaper, try one of the jobs pages on the Net.) Now elicit a selection of popular jobs and discuss what skills and personal qualities are necessary for each one.

Online

The Career Key website is an American college site which tries to help students find the right career. There are numerous approaches, but a good place to start is with the personality quiz. Once this is done, students are invited to look at jobs which may suit them. If you have already done work on character, go directly to the Jobs That Fit My Personality section. Give students a chance to work through the material and come up with a selection of jobs they think may suit them.

Offline

Use the *Ideal job* activity to follow up on the online work. This will need adapting for adults who are already working. You could concentrate on the jobs they are doing now and the ones recommended on the website. What would they do if they could choose any job?

Follow-ups / Variations

Play a game with students asking questions to establish the occupation of one member of the class. Questions can only be answered with 'yes' or 'no'. This can also be done using mime with the student doing a short visual representation of their job before taking questions.

Alternatively use a selection of job pictures, letting a student decide on one and describing the qualities needed to do the job. The rest of the class has to guess which picture is being described. This is also an ideal opportunity to do work on daily routine.

Ideal job

Think about the questions below and make some notes:

- What jobs do you think you would like to do?
- What qualities are needed for them?
- What did you find out on the Career Key website …
  – about your personality?
  – about recommended jobs?
- Have you changed your mind after using the Career Key?
- Which of the recommended jobs interests you most?
- What do you think a typical day in this job would be like?

© Cambridge University Press 2000

2.25 Cooking with kids

Summary: Recipes for young people

Level: Elementary and above

Time: 1 hour (15 minutes on the Net)

Language: Food vocabulary, describing processes, likes and dislikes

Sites: http://www.inmotion-pcs.com/amass/theboss/recipe.htm

Notes: These recipes use American English vocabulary, so if you are teaching in a British English context, you may have to do some work on the UK–US vocabulary differences (see *Activity 2.16 The same language*).

Preparation

Food and drink vocabulary is one of the areas which young learners usually cover in depth. Take time out now to do some revision of fruit, vegetables, drinks, etc. Brainstorm the vocabulary onto the board in various categories. Do the *Some of my favourite things* activity. This is also an opportunity to do some work on expressing likes and dislikes. Get some feedback as a class, and make a top ten food and drink chart based on their preferences.

79

Online

There are lots of recipes for kids on the Recipe Collection page, divided into various categories. They have fun names and are often very colourful and easy to make. Make a questionnaire, e.g. What vegetables are on the Individual Pizzas? or Why is a Purple Cow purple? Be careful to choose easy recipes and questions.

Offline

Take feedback on the questionnaire and clear up any problems which have arisen. Now have a competition to design the most exotic sandwich, or the strangest drink. Encourage students to write a description of how to make the food or drink, to draw an illustration and to think of a fun name for it.

Follow-ups / Variations

If you're truly adventurous and have the facilities, you could try producing some of the recipes in class – or maybe have a fun food competition with everyone making something at home and bringing it into class for a party.

Some of my favourite things

Complete the sentences about food and drink ...

My favourite drink is ....
My favourite food is..
I love..
I hate ....
I never eat...
For breakfast I usually have ....
I usually have lunch at..
My perfect dinner is..

Now ask your partner questions about food and drink.

© Cambridge University Press 2000

80

2.26 **Playing it safe**

Summary: Finding out about Internet security

Level: Elementary and above

Time: 1 hour (15 minutes on the Net)

Language: Imperatives, advice

Sites: http://www.worldkids.net/school/safety/internet

Notes: The Internet has plenty of questionable material, and – as in real life – has users who are all-too-willing to take advantage of young people. This is a valuable lesson for young people on the dos and don'ts of Internet life.

Preparation

Start with a general discussion of computer usage, perhaps using the *TechnoKids* activity. Find out as a class who has a computer and what they use it for. Who plays games, and what kind of games do they play? Who has access to the Internet at home, and what do they use it for? You could also try eliciting what some of the dangers or problems with using the Internet might be before leading in to the *Online* stage.

Online

Give students time to look through the safety tips and make notes to summarise them later. You might want to set a small comprehension task to go with the reading.

Offline

Discuss the safety tips put forward. Which are the most important ones, and which ones do they think are unimportant. Are there any they don't understand? Is there any information they think should be added?

Draw up a set of rules for Internet use in the classroom. Negotiate with the class. This can become a useful contract for general computer use behaviour during the course.

TechnoKids

Talking about computers:

- Have you got a computer at home?
  - What do you use it for?
  - Do you play computer games? (what kind of games?)
  - Do you use it for homework? (how do you use it?)
- Have you got Internet access at home?
  - What do you use it for?
  - Do you use email? (who do you write to?)
  - Do you look at webpages? (what kind of webpages?)
- Do you think you use your computer too much?

© Cambridge University Press 2000

2.27 Olympic Games

Summary: Finding out about the Olympic Games

Level: Mid-intermediate and above

Time: 1 hour (25 minutes on the Net)

Language: Sports vocabulary, mixed tenses (past)

Sites: http://www.aafla.com/OlympicInformationCenter/

Notes: The Olympic Primer section has lots of useful information about the Games. The site also has Web Games and reports on Olympic cities.

Preparation

If the Games have ever been held in the country / city where you teach, you have an ideal opportunity to introduce the topic. What happened during the Games? Were they good or bad for the country / city? How did the image of the country / city change after the Games? If this is not the case, simply move straight into eliciting information about the Games. What does the class know about them, and what would they like to know?

Online

Using the *Just a Game* activity, visit the Olympic Primer site and give students a chance to answer the questions as well as to look for the information from the *Preparation* stage of the activity.

Offline

Get feedback on the questionnaire and on the information from the *Preparation* stage. Were they surprised by anything they read? Imagine that the Games are going to be held in their city (assuming that they haven't been already!). What improvements would they have to make? Plan what should be done, and design a logo and mascot for the games. This could also be turned into an extended project as suggested in *Follow-ups/Variations*.

Follow-ups / Variations

Students design a bid for the city you live in. Why should the Games come there? This could be built up into a web-based project (see *Section 3* for ideas).

Just a game

What do you know about the Olympic Games?

Where and when did the Games start?
How often do they take place?
Who revived the Olympic Games, and when?
Where are the Games being held next?
Where is the International Olympic Committee based?
What is the Olympic symbol, and what does it signify?
Can you name three Olympic mascots?
Which country first televised the Olympics? In which year?
What is doping?
Why were the 1936 Games controversial?

© Cambridge University Press 2000

2.28 The London sightseeing tour (2)

Summary: Planning a day out in London

Level: Lower-intermediate and above

Time: 1 hour (30 minutes on the Net) ~~time,~~ *day schedule*

Language: Making arrangements, suggesting, agreeing, disagreeing

Sites: http://www.londontown.com

Notes: Most major world cities have plenty of websites devoted to them. Look in Yahoo! for a city which suits you and your students best. This activity works well in a business English class.

Preparation

Start off with a general chat about London. Have any of the students visited the city? What did they do there? What did they visit and see? Get students into groups of three and four and give them time to talk to each other and find out what they like doing when they visit a new city. Do they like seeing monuments, going shopping, visiting galleries, etc.? Now tell them they are going to plan a day out in London, between them, and that they must try to agree on what to see and do and to accommodate the likes and dislikes of each member of the group.

Online

The London Town website has complete coverage of things to see and do in London. Steer students towards sections such as Attractions, Open Top Bus Tours, Sightseeing and Walking Tours. There are also sections on eating, shopping, etc.

Offline

Once they have agreed, get them to complete the *London sightseeing tour* worksheet. Re-distribute the group members to make new groups with everyone explaining to the others what their group decided to do, where to go, etc. If you have paper maps of the city or other realia, these can make the activity more interesting. For those with unlimited Internet time, stay with the computers for a more interesting description, using the website.

Follow-ups / Variations

A logical follow-up is to design a similar resource for the city your students live in. Decide on the major features of the city. Why would someone want to visit it, and what should they do while there? What other information would they need to know to have a successful visit?

London sightseeing tour

Write a brief summary of times and activities as you plan them.

8 am – breakfast in the hotel
9 am – ....
10 am – ....
11 am – ....
12 pm – ....
1 pm – ....
2 pm – ....
3 pm – ....
4 pm – ....
5 pm – ....
6 pm – ....
7 pm – ....
8 pm – ....

© Cambridge University Press 2000

2.29 What's the time?   (3)

Summary: Talking about the time around the world

Level: Elementary and above (young learners)

Time: 40 minutes (10 minutes on the Net)

Language: The time

Sites: http://fang.fa.gau.hu/~rpapp/scripts/worldclo.html

Notes: There are plenty of time sites. I use this one because it's easy to work with and very quick, but you could also try http://www.bsdi.com/date

Preparation

This works well as a revision activity for telling the time. Make sure you do some pre-teaching or reminding before visiting the website.

Online

Distribute the **What's the time?** activity and give students time on the website to answer the questions. Bear in mind that most of the times noted from the website will only vary by a few minutes, so this activity alone will not practise the full range of times you might want to cover.

Offline

In pairs, students ask and answer from the **What's the time?** activity. Move on to a more personalised activity with students talking to each other about their daily routines. This can then be turned into a writing activity focussing on the student's daily routine.

Follow-ups / Variations

You can also do some work on nationalities and countries using the webpage. A slightly more complex activity would be to quiz students by country, rather than by city. They would then have to use their search skills to find out which cities on the time page are from which country, before being able to answer the time questions. To get a full range of times to practise, visit a TV company page and make a similar activity with the TV listings page, basing the questions around the formula: What time is the news on TVE1?, etc.

What's the time?

Find out the time in these places.   Find out the time in these places.

STUDENT A   STUDENT B

Amsterdam.................................   Osaka..
Taipei .... Sydney.......................................
Stockholm.................................   San Francisco ....
Rome.......................................   Rio de Janeiro ....

© Cambridge University Press 2000

New York	Moscow ....
Mexico City	Hong Kong ....
Now ask your partner about ...	Now ask your partner about ...
Osaka.......................................	Amsterdam ....
Sydney	Taipei.......................................
San Francisco	Stockholm...............................
Rio de Janeiro	Rome.......................................
Moscow	New York................................
Hong Kong...............................	Mexico City ....

© Cambridge University Press 2000

2.30 Dream holiday

Summary: Planning the perfect holiday

Level: Upper-intermediate and above

Time: 1 hour (30 minutes on the Net)

Language: Talking about holidays and travel plans

Sites: http://www.lonelyplanet.com

Notes: It's worth noting that the Lonely Planet website accompanies a range of extremely authoritative and useful printed books. Another good site is at http://travel.roughguides.com – which has the full texts from all their publications online.

Preparation

Start off with a simple questionnaire on holiday preferences. Get feedback as a class and give students the opportunity to talk to anyone who may have been to a country they would like to visit themselves.

Online

Tell the class that money is no object and that they can go where they want and travel how they want. They have one month of holiday to organise. They must take care of deciding where they are going, how they are going to travel, what they'll do when they are there, etc.

Offline

Students form small groups and tell each other about their dream holiday. They can also inform their colleagues about the climate, geography, food and culture of their chosen destination(s).

Follow-ups / Variations

This activity can be extended further with more detailed planning of the travel arrangements including looking for airline tickets and finding out train and coach details. (A good place to start is the Yahoo! travel section.)

Dream holiday

Think about these questions, then get into groups and discuss them.

- What would your dream holiday be?
- Where would you like to go?
- What would you do?
- Who would you go with?
- How would you travel?

© Cambridge University Press 2000

2.31 A night at the movies

Summary: Planning a night out at the movies

Level: Mid-intermediate and above

Time: 1 hour (30 minutes on the Net)

Language: Likes and dislikes, cinema vocabulary, arranging to go out

Sites: http://www.cinemachine.com

Notes: You can also try http://www.corona.bc.ca/films/filmlistings.html Another good site for movie reviews is at http://www.cinepad.com/awards/ These sites use 'movie' and 'film' interchangeably – make sure your students are aware of this practice.

Preparation

The *Movie crossword* handout is a good starting point for this activity, as it activates a lot of the vocabulary which will be needed in the following parts. Students then walk round finding out who likes which types of films. They need to get together into small groups with others who like the same kind of films before moving on to the *Online* section of the activity.

Online

CineMachine has reviews of forthcoming and recent releases, while the Film Listings site can be searched in many ways: by genre, by name, by date, etc. Give students time to see which films are on at the cinema, and to decide which one they would like to see. Encourage negotiation during this part. Further investigation can be done online to find out where the films are on and to arrange which cinema to go to, and at what time.

Offline

Get feedback as a group, exchanging experiences and decisions. I usually like to follow this activity up with a look at the Cine Pad top 100 films of all time website. This can easily be turned into an information gap activity if printed out. (Take the top twenty films and make two copies of the lists, then blank out the titles – fully or partially – of half the films on each copy. Students then see which titles they can complete (or guess) and ask their partner questions to fill the gaps on their copy.)

You can also use this site as a springboard for students to make a personal (or class) list of their top ten films of all time. They might start by deleting all the ones they have never heard of, then get into groups to strike off any of those they think are not very good before finally choosing ten from the remaining titles.

Follow-ups / Variations

Film titles are often wildly changed when they are translated into other languages. *The Sound of Music*, for example, was called Sonrisas y Lágrimas (Smiles and Tears) in Spain. A good activity is a matching exercise with original titles and the titles from the country where you are teaching.

A written assignment of a film review is another good activity to round off this cinema class.

Movie crossword

ACROSS
1) Animated films (8)
4) A type of film involving a journey (4,5)
6) Famous kung fu actor (5,3)
11) Film award (5)
13) You need to buy this to see a film (6)
14) You make a film with a ... ... (6)
16) Do you want to go ... the cinema? (2)
17) What's on ... the cinema tonight? (2)
18) Film with cowboys and Indians (7)
19) Are there any good films ... tonight? (2)
21) An exciting kind of film (8)
22) Text on screen in a foreign language film (8)
23) Explosions, fights, battles ... (7,7)

DOWN
2) Male performer in a film (5)
3) Where most science fiction films are set (5)
4) Round metal container for film (4)
5) Filmed ... in Africa (2,8)
6) Old films were made in ... (5,3,5)
7) Frightening type of film (6)
8) You eat this in the cinema (7)
9) Famous film alien (1,1)
10) Short advert for a film (7)
12) A funny film (6)
15) *Alien* was set on a ... (9)
16) There's one ... woman in the film. It's definitely a very male story (5)
20) The story of a film (4)

© Cambridge University Press 2000

KEY: ACROSS – 1 cartoons, 4 road movie, 6 Bruce Lee, 11 Oscar, 13 ticket, 14 camera, 16 to, 17 at, 18 western, 19 on, 21 thriller, 22 subtitles, 23 special effects
DOWN – 2 actor, 3 space, 4 reel, 5 on location, 6 black and white, 7 horror, 8 popcorn, 9 ET, 10 trailer, 12 comedy, 15 spaceship, 16 token, 20 plot

2.32 Classified ads

Summary: Buying online

Level: Advanced and above

Time: 1 hour (30 minutes on the Net)

Language: Describing things

Sites: http://www.loot.com

Notes: Another good classifieds site is at http://www.nettrader.co.uk
Classified adverts use a lot of shorthand and abbreviations,
so you may want to do some work on these before visiting
the site. If Christmas is not culturally appropriate in your
teaching situation, you can easily adapt the activity to a
more suitable occasion.

Preparation

Students complete the ***Christmas shopping*** questionnaire, individually, then
in pairs. Then get feedback as a group. Now tell students they have a certain
amount of money to buy presents for their family and that this year they are
going to do their shopping online.

Online

Loot has an extremely efficient search facility, so it will be easy for students
to find what they are looking for this way. Alternatively, they can browse one
of the sections until they find what they are looking for (e.g. transport, computers, sound and vision). The idea here is to fill up their shopping list within
budget.

Offline

In groups students explain what they have bought, how much they paid for
each item and who it is for. They should try to explain why they think each
item is suitable for the person they are going to give it to.

Follow-ups / Variations

A good follow-up is to organise an unwanted gift swap. Give out two or three pictures of gifts to each student and explain they got them for Christmas (or whichever holiday you are working on) and now they don't want them. Old catalogues or magazines are a good source of useful pictures for this type of activity.) Have them write up small ads for each of the products, with descriptions and prices. Then students walk round bartering with each other to exchange what they have for things they really want.

Christmas shopping

Think about these questions and make some notes.

What do you usually get for Christmas?
What would you like to get for Christmas?
Do you enjoy shopping for presents for other people?
Do you enjoy buying things for yourself?
Who do you usually buy presents for?
What did you buy them last time?
If you could buy them anything, what would you buy?
Write the names of the people you usually buy presents for and then
   make a list of what you would buy them if you could.

© Cambridge University Press 2000

2.33 Finding a flat

Summary: Shopping for a new home online

Level: Upper-intermediate and above

Time: 1 hour (30 minutes on the Net)

Language: Describing houses and homes

Sites: http://www.homefileuk.co.uk

Notes: Also worth trying are Bushells at http://www.bushells.com
   which has photos to go with the adverts and
   http://www.nettrader.co.uk/property/residential/ which deals more
   with rentals. These sites also deal with commercial
   properties, so can be used in a business English context.
   (See also *Activity 2.48 Dream houses*.)

Preparation

Get students talking about where they live and what they think makes a good home. Get feedback as a group. Each student should imagine that they are going to London, either to study, or to work, some in low-paid jobs, others in well-paid jobs. Each of them should be told how much money they have, what they are going to be doing, where they will be working or studying and whether they should be looking for a rental or to buy somewhere. You can use the map at the HomeFileUK site to find suitable areas.

Online

Using the tasks they have been given, students have to find a suitable property either to rent or to buy. They must try to find something in the area in which they are going to work.

Offline

Get students in small groups to tell each other what they have found and to describe their new homes.

Follow-ups / Variations

Get students to write a letter from their new home, describing it and the surrounding area to friends or family. It provides good practice of all the vocabulary encountered during the actual activity. For lower levels, you could use the online estate agents offices to practise furniture vocabulary as well as *it has got, there is* and *there are*.

2.34 Suits you

Summary: Talking about clothing and fashion
Level: Elementary and above
Time: 1 hour (30 minutes on the Net)
Language: Vocabulary connected with clothing and fashion
Sites: http://www.gap.com
Notes: Also http://www.diesel.co.uk

Preparation

With lower levels, you'll need to pre-teach the clothing vocabulary you intend to focus on. With higher levels, start with the *Fashion* speaking activity. Make sure all the vocabulary you'll need for the *Online* activity comes out in this part of the class.

Online

Included here are two examples of online clothes shops – you can choose the male or female section and look at their collections. Lower levels can use the pictures as visual cues for descriptions which can be oral or written up later. Higher levels should go on a virtual shopping trip, with students finding clothes they like the look of and inviting opinion from the others, just as in a real shopping trip.

Follow-ups / Variations

An alternative start activity is to have students do a walkround of some kind (e.g. a Find Someone Who ... activity) then put them in pairs back-to-back and have them describe what the other is wearing.

As a follow-up, with lower levels and young learners, cut-out items of clothing can be used to dress sketches of people and then students describe them, 'Susan is wearing ...'.

Teenagers can organise a fashion show, with people taking it in turns to announce who is on the 'catwalk' and what they are wearing, describing everything as if it's the latest fashion. It's a good idea for the teacher to have first go, just to 'break the ice'!

> **Fashion**
>
> **Are you worried about fashion and trends?**
>
> - What's your favourite outfit for work / school? What about at the weekend?
> - What do you wear when you go out socially?
> - What do you wear around the house?

© Cambridge University Press 2000

- Which of these things would you wear, and which wouldn't you wear?

Flared jeans	A checked shirt	A fur coat
A waistcoat	A flowery shirt	A three-piece suit
High-heeled shoes	Thigh-length boots	Striped trousers
A kipper tie	Cowboy boots	A mini-skirt
A denim jacket	Torn jeans	A woolly hat
Stockings	A sweatshirt	A cardigan

© Cambridge University Press 2000

2.35 A fine day out

Summary: Getting travel information

Level: Mid-intermediate and above

Time: 1 hour (20 minutes on the Net)

Language: Times and timetables / travel information

Sites: http://www.pti.org.uk/

Notes: The UK Public Transport Information site has links to all major travel organisations in the UK, including airlines, train companies, coach and bus companies, etc. Some of these services (for example, The Train Line, which allows online booking of train tickets) require you to register before using them. Registration is free, but it's a good idea to do it before the class.

This activity is easily adapted to other countries, using the Yahoo! Travel section as a starting point for finding resources.

Preparation

This is an ideal opportunity to do some work on travel vocabulary so do the *Travel tips* activity as a warm-up. At lower levels, concentrate on the prepositions (by train, on foot, etc.). With higher levels, focus on the problem area of trip, excursion, voyage, journey, etc.

Online

Give out a set of tasks concerning finding train times, plane times, prices, etc. Students should be asking questions such as, *How much is a return ticket from London to Edinburgh? What time does the first coach to Bristol leave? Is it cheaper to fly or get the train from London to Edinburgh?* This is best done as an 'interactive reading race' in teams. You write out the questions on separate slips of paper and place them in one pile which all students can *competitive* reach easily. Students take a question and look for the answer before returning it and taking another. This process is repeated until all the questions have been answered.

If you don't like the idea of making this kind of exercise too competitive, simply introduce a time limit to the activity, with students finding as many answers as possible within the given time frame.

Follow-ups / Variations

This can be set up as a typical travel agent scenario with some students having the tasks and other students being travel agents using the Net to get the information. As the travel agents will be very busy, encourage the customers to make small talk as they sit waiting for the answers – just like in real life!

Travel tips

How do you like to travel?
How do you usually travel during the week?
And at the weekend?
Do you prefer a car or bicycle to public transport? Why?
How do you travel when you go on holiday?
What's the longest flight you've ever been on?
What about the longest boat trip / train or coach journey?

Now get into small groups and compare your answers.

© Cambridge University Press 2000

2.36 But is it art?

Summary: Talking about art

Level: Upper-intermediate and above

Time: 1 hour (30 minutes on the Net)

Language: Describing things, giving opinions, biographies

Sites: http://www.artsearch.net   *Canada gallery*

Notes: Art Search is the gateway to an enormous collection of web resources connected with art, galleries, artists.

Preparation

You need a set of postcards or colour photocopies of famous paintings by famous people. You might even like to invite each student to bring in a post-card or magazine cut-out showing a painting. Give students a chance to walk round examining them, but don't let them see any details yet – just the picture. Get students into pairs and ask each pair to choose a picture they particularly like. Pre-teach some vocabulary for describing pictures (e.g. 'in the foreground', 'in the background', 'on the horizon').   *Vocab*

Online

Starting at the Art Search page, ask each pair to find out some information about the picture they have chosen, and the artist who painted it. They should get biographical information, history of the picture and details of other work done by the artist.

Offline

Each of the pairs is now in charge of a special exhibition in the class. Their job is to give a small introduction to the exhibition, talking about their chosen painting and giving some background information on the artist.

Follow-ups / Variations

A written description of one of the postcards is a good activity.

A simple alternative introduction to the task involves dividing the class into pairs and giving each member of the pair a simple sketch to describe to their partner, who has to draw it.

2.37 Puzzlemaker

Summary: Making and solving puzzles

Level: Elementary and above (young learners)

Time: 1 hour (30 minutes on the Net)

Language: Vocabulary revision

Sites: http://www.puzzlemaker.com

Notes: Puzzlemaker is a real timesaver for busy teachers, but is also fun for students to use. It makes all kinds of puzzles which can then be printed and used in class or for homework. Puzzles include: wordsearches, wordsearches with hidden messages, crosswords, cryptograms, etc.

Preparation

There are lots of different ways of using Puzzlemaker, but it's particularly useful as a regular vocabulary revision activity. This is an idea for using the wordsearch maker. Get students into pairs to brainstorm vocabulary for a particular area you have been working on, e.g. food and drink, travel or similar. Have them make a list of 15–20 words they can remember from the field.

Online

Show them how to use the wordsearch maker. All they then have to do is fill in the form and the webpage makes their wordsearch for them. Encourage them to personalise the title. Make sure you print a copy of each quiz when it is finished.

Offline

Photocopy the quizzes and distribute them over the following classes, either as quick activities in class or for homework. I like to use this regularly as it gives the students some investment in the work done in class, and there's the added challenge of being able to make a puzzle which can't be solved by their colleagues.

Follow-ups / Variations

Investigate the other types of puzzles – most of them are easy to make, and once your students have learnt each type they will be able to make them unsupervised.

Gavin's Fruit Wordsearch

G	T	T	C	F	J	R	A	U	C	D	K	E	V	S
O	L	I	R	P	Y	O	E	Q	I	H	F	E	E	N
R	K	J	U	M	B	U	Q	P	A	Z	E	X	J	K
A	F	L	L	R	J	Z	K	Y	E	X	N	R	I	P
N	B	V	A	L	F	A	T	N	P	F	I	H	R	H
G	O	E	G	A	A	E	I	C	A	S	R	A	O	Y
E	T	Z	N	V	D	R	P	M	R	U	E	Z	L	P
J	M	F	Q	U	A	Q	W	A	G	P	G	W	T	I
X	Q	V	E	D	R	N	U	O	R	H	N	I	F	B
V	W	B	N	I	Y	P	Y	U	L	G	A	U	C	O
Q	Z	A	O	A	N	O	L	E	M	P	T	U	F	E
Z	M	B	P	F	X	U	Y	V	G	E	M	L	G	B
N	N	P	K	S	S	S	Z	Z	F	S	U	I	Z	X
V	L	P	I	W	L	O	J	B	A	N	A	N	A	G

PRUNE	ORANGE	MANDARIN	PEAR
GRAPE	BANANA	TANGERINE	
MELON	GRAPEFRUIT	CHERRY	

2.38 Holiday posters

Summary: Making posters for celebrations

Level: Elementary and above

Time: 1 hour (15 minutes on the Net)

Language: Vocabulary for parties and celebrations

Sites: http://www.kidsdomain.com/clip/

Notes: Also http://www.yahooligans.com/content/tg/clipart.html This idea can be used to coincide with major festivals such as Christmas, Easter, Bonfire night, or local celebrations in your city or country.

Preparation

Have a look at some good posters in class. What do students think makes a good poster? Then get students to do a rough sketch of what they would like to put on their posters.

Online

Use one of the clipart galleries above to find suitable pictures for the posters. Make sure you save any useful pictures by right clicking on them and choosing *Save Picture As* ... . (Remember where you save them!)

Offline

Work with the students to produce their posters using a word processor and a program such as Microsoft Word and the pictures they have saved from the Net. For very young learners, Microsoft produces a word processor called Creative Writer which can be used easily to make posters, invitations and cards.

Follow-ups / Variations

There are plenty of clipart collections on the Net, and you can find themed sets of pictures for most areas of life (try searching at Yahoo! for 'free clipart' or 'clipart collection').

100

Adapt this activity to higher levels, with posters for pop concerts, theatre events, etc. Business English classes can work on new ad campaigns for their companies, or logo designs.

Business

HALLOWE'EN PARTY!
TOMORROW @ 8 IN THE CAFÉ

2.39 Nice day today

Summary: Talking about the weather

Level: Elementary and above

Time: 1 hour (15 minutes on the Net)

Language: Weather vocabulary and structures

Sites: http://weather.yahoo.com

Notes: See also *Activity 2.9 The weather*

Preparation

The Yahoo! weather site uses the standard symbols for rain, cloud, storm, etc. Print these out (or draw your own) and use them to pre-teach or revise ways of talking about the weather (don't forget to do work on the difference between 'it's rainy' and 'it's raining', etc.).

Online

This is a simple ask and answer activity with students looking for details of the weather in various locations around the world and then asking their partner about other places. Give them time to find the places and make notes before leaving the computers

Offline

Students complete the **Weather forecast** activity.

Follow-ups / Variations

A world map can make a nice addition to this activity, especially for younger learners. As they ask and answer questions about the weather, they can draw the appropriate symbols on the weather map. This is also a good opportunity to do some work on country names.

For higher levels, use the long-range forecast from the Yahoo! page for the country where you live and have students pretend to be weather forecasters on the TV. If you can, put a sketch of the country on the board and get them to stick weather symbols on it as they deliver the forecast.

Weather forecast

Find out what the weather is like in …	Find out what the weather is like in …
Student A	Student B
London	Rome
Mexico City	Reykjavik

© Cambridge University Press 2000

Sydney	Buenos Aires
New York	Moscow
Cairo	Toronto
Berlin	Tokyo

Now ask your partner about …	**Now ask your partner about …**
Rome	London
Reykjavik	Mexico City
Buenos Aires	Sydney
Moscow	New York
Toronto	Cairo
Tokyo	Berlin

2.40 Disaster area

Summary: Talking about world problems

Level: Advanced

Time: 1 hour (30 minutes on the Net)

Language: Global issues

Sites: http://dir.yahoo.com/Society_and_Culture/Issues_and_Causes/

Notes: This is a wide area for investigation and plenty of time will be needed to find really useful information.

Preparation

Give each student time to complete the *Disaster area* debate, then make pairs and have them negotiate a new order and compare their answers to the last two points. Gradually combine the groups until the whole class has decided on a final order for the problems. Divide the class into four groups and distribute the top four problems, one to each group.

Online

The idea here is for each group to get as much information as possible about the theme they have been given: the size and importance of the problem, principal countries affected, the global implications of the problem.

Offline

Students should do a presentation of the material they have found. When all the presentations have been done, a vote should be taken on which cause to support. Students can then use the Internet for further investigation into how to do something to help. For example, the Hunger Page at www.thehungersite.com donates money for food to starving countries every time a link is clicked from their site. This is financed by large institutions and could become a daily visit for your class.

Follow-ups / Variations

This whole area would make an ideal vehicle for an extended web project (see *Section 3*).

Disaster area

Here are various problems the world faces. Put them in order according to how important you think they are.

☐ Famine   ☐ Destruction of the ozone layer
☐ Poverty   ☐ Greenhouse effect
☐ Over-population   ☐ Pollution
☐ Deforestation   ☐ Desertification
☐ War   ☐ Disease

Can you add any more to the list?

Do you think any of them are related to each other?

© Cambridge University Press 2000

2.41 Kids make the news

Summary: Writing and publishing for an audience

Level: Elementary and above

Time: 1 hour (15 minutes on the Net)

Language: All

Sites: http://www.kidnews.com/news.html

Notes: This site publishes writing by kids from around the world. Note that not everything sent to Kid News will be published, so it's important to point this out and make alternative arrangements for a display of the work done – perhaps as a poster in the classroom.

Preparation

Find five or six easy stories from the Kid News site which are suitable for your class and level. Organise a walk-round comprehension activity or reading race with questions stuck on the walls and articles spread around the class – students have to find the questions on the walls and then walk round trying to find which article they refer to, and then answer them. This activity can easily be adapted for the *Online* part of the class, making it a more interactive Net-based activity.

Online

Give students a chance to look round the site and see for themselves what kind of stories are there, how they are presented, etc.

Offline

Brainstorm some interesting or unusual events that have happened locally, then divide the class into groups and assign one event to each group. Give plenty of time for students to prepare their stories before sending them off to the website.

Follow-ups / Variations

As a follow-up, print the stories and have the students illustrate them, either with their own drawings, or with pictures from magazines and newspapers. Then organise an exhibition of the work.

2.42 It's a mystery

> **Summary:** Secret codes
>
> **Level:** Elementary and above
>
> **Time:** 1 hour (20 minutes on the Net)
>
> **Language:** Numbers, the alphabet
>
> **Sites:** http://www.bonus.com/bonus/card/Enigma_Machine.html
>
> **Notes:** http://www.iut.univ-paris8.fr/~rosmord/nomhiero.html will convert names written normally into their hieroglyphic equivalents. For more code sites try http://ink.yahoo.com/bin/query?p=write+secret+messages&hc=0&hs=38

Preparation

You'll need to pre-teach the numbers 1–26 and the letters of the alphabet or do some revision of them if your students are already familiar with them. I like to do alphabet races round the class to quickly revise the alphabet. Games such as bingo are excellent for number revision.

Write the letters of the alphabet on the board, then write the numbers underneath, '1' below 'A', '2' below 'B', etc. Write a simple sentence on the board using numbers (something like My name is Gavin which would be: 13 25 14 1 13 5 9 19 7 1 22 9 13) and get students to tell you the correct letter for each number until they have discovered the message. Now do the **Secret messages** activity, with student A dictating their numbers and student B writing in the number and saying the corresponding letter until they discover the words. Change the words I have used to suit your group.

Online

Bonus Com features a working model of the Enigma Machine – a code maker and breaker from the Second World War. Give students a chance to set their code and encode a short message to someone else in the class before passing on the message and the key. Recipients of a coded message should set the machine up and decode the message.

Follow-ups / Variations

Get students to invent their own codes. Show them how to invert the numbers so that the alphabet-number code is also inverted, or to skip a number so that A becomes 1, B becomes 3, etc. Once they have invented a code, other students can have fun trying to break it.

If you use the hieroglyphic website (see **Notes**), ask students if they like how their name looks in ancient hieroglyphics and invite them to improve on it by drawing their own symbols to represent their name.

Secret messages

Student A	*Student B*
Birthday (2 9 _ _ _ _ _ _)	(_ _ _ _ _ _ _ _)............................
(_ _ _ _ _ _)	School (19 3 _ _ _ _)
Bedroom (_ _ _ _ _ _ _)	(_ _ _ _ _ _ _)............................
(_ _ _ _ _ _ _ _ _ _)	Television (_ _ _ _ _ _ _ _ _ _)
Sandwich (_ _ _ _ _ _ _ _)	(_ _ _ _ _ _ _ _)............................
(_ _ _ _ _ _ _)..............................	Bicycle (_ _ _ _ _ _ _)
Football (_ _ _ _ _ _ _ _)	(_ _ _ _ _ _ _ _)............................
(_ _ _ _ _ _ _ _)............................	Armchair (_ _ _ _ _ _ _ _)

2.43 Australian wildlife

Summary: Finding out about animal life in Australia

Level: Elementary and above

Time: 1 hour (15 minutes on the Net)

Language: Facts and figures, colours, habits

Sites: http://www.worldkids.net/critters/marsupials/

Notes: Similar sites can be found at http://www.aaa.com.au/A_Z/a.shtml and http://sun.kent.wednet.edu/KSD/DE/st_proj/australia/australia.html

Preparation

Start by eliciting some information about Australia. If the subject of animal life doesn't come out, introduce the theme. Do students know any Australian animals? If so, get some information on the board.

Online

There are plenty of pages on the Marsupial Museum page, each one dealing with a different animal (note that not all marsupials come from Australia). Each page has at least one picture, and some information about the animal. The language is not difficult here, but you will need to be prepared for some problems. A controlled reading task is the best way of approaching this. The *Animal facts* worksheet is designed for this. Give pairs of students one animal to investigate. Younger students can also be encouraged to draw the animal they see on the page, or colour in a picture of it (see *Follow-ups / Variations*).

Offline

Use the information you have gathered to make a gallery of Australian animals. Get students to illustrate the *Animal facts* worksheet with a picture of the animal in question.

Follow-ups / Variations

As a preliminary activity for the website, try printing out pictures of the animals you want to study, and having students label the pictures with the names of the animals.

A follow-up project could be done on the animal life where you teach; this could even become a web project. Another quick follow-up activity is to make a wordsearch with the animal names. (See **Activity 2.37 Puzzlemaker.**)

Animal facts

Fill in the grid with the information you find:

Name of animal	
Colour	
Size	
Food	
Habits	

© Cambridge University Press 2000

2.44 Theme park

Summary: Touring Disneyland, designing a theme park

Level: Mid-intermediate and above

Time: 1 hour (20 minutes on the Net)

Language: Descriptions, agreeing and disagreeing, making suggestions.

Sites: http://dlpfan.org/int/s7007.htm

Notes: This Virtual Tour site has very detailed visuals of all the different parts of the park. See also the official Disney pages at http://www.disney.com

Preparation

A general class discussion on theme parks and days out is a good start. What can you do if you want a day out where you live? Has anyone been to Disneyland? What kinds of rides do people like?

Online

There are five principal parts to the Disneyland website (Mainstreet USA, Frontierland, Adventureland, Fantasyland, Discoveryland) modelled on the original in America. Divide the class into five groups and give them one part each. As they look around their part of the park they need to decide what they would like to do there. Ask them to make notes on the various activities.

Offline

Redistribute the students into different groups, ensuring that each group has at least one member from each of the original five groups. Now tell them that they have won a weekend away at Disneyland and that they have to organise what they are going to do. When they have mapped out their two-day stay at the theme park, they give other groups a rundown of what they would do. Encourage comment and discussion on the best way to spend the two days.

Follow-ups / Variations

An excellent follow-up is a 'design your own theme park' project. Students design a theme park which reflects their culture as well as their favourite rides. In a mixed nationality class, each student can contribute a ride or show from their country.

2.45 Computer detectives

> **Summary:**   Solving mysteries
>
> **Level:**   Upper-intermediate and above
>
> **Time:**   75 minutes (25 minutes on the Net)

Language: Predictions, reasoning, giving explanations

Sites: http://www.thecase.com

Notes: Young learners can join in at http://www.thecase.com/kids/ or
the Nancy Drew page: http://www.nancydrew.com/kids/
Extra ideas on working with mysteries at
http://www.mysterynet.com/learn/lessonplans/main.html

Preparation

Start off with a mystery of your own. My favourite is to describe the following scene: 'There is a man in the middle of a field; he is dead and has an
unopened package next to him. What happened?' Students are only allowed
to ask questions which can be answered with 'yes' or 'no'. The answer is that
he jumped from a plane, and the unopened package is his parachute. This is
also a good opportunity to do some work on prediction, encouraging students to talk among themselves: 'he might have been …', 'perhaps he was …',
etc.

Online

The Case has weekly and daily mysteries, so you'll have to look at
the website just before you do the class. The See-N-Solve section
(http//www.thecase.com/see/) has a crime story with a picture of the crime scene,
so both textual and visual clues play a part. Choose a mystery and give students time to read it and discuss the clues before they take a look at the solution.

Offline

Examine how a typical mystery story is put together, trying to identify key
parts: set the scene, introduce the characters, drop in a couple of clues to the
identity of the criminal, the solution.
   Use the picture from the Writing Contest (http//www.thecase.com/photo/) to
create group mystery stories, or supply pictures yourself from magazines or
newspapers.

Follow-ups / Variations

In the **Preparation** stage, encourage students to participate with mysteries of their own. Alternatively, put them in pairs and invite them to make up their own mystery stories.

2.46 Who said that ... ?

> **Summary:** Famous quotations
>
> **Level:** Upper-intermediate and above
>
> **Time:** 75 minutes (30 minutes on the Net)
>
> **Language:** Talking about famous people
>
> **Sites:** http://www.famous-quotations.com/
>
> **Notes:** This site can be searched alphabetically, by category and by author. More quotation sites are available through Yahoo! if you don't find what you are looking for here.

Preparation

Start with the **Who said that ... ?** activity. There's a good chance that your students will know some of them, but not all. Get feedback and see which ones they know, and what they know about the people who said them, and the circumstances in which they were said.

An alternative presentation might be to start by putting the names of the people from the **Who said that ... ?** activity up on the board. Elicit any information about the people, and see if the students know what they are famous for. Then lead into the main activity.

Online

Give them time to finish the activity, finding the quotes they didn't know. Encourage quick finishers to look around, pointing out the different search options. Get feedback on the rest of the answers. Now tell them they are going to make an inspirational quotations wall, and that they have ten minutes to find two or three quotations each which they think are useful, funny, intelligent, etc.

Offline

Using large pieces of card or paper, have students make the quotations wall, discussing how quotations should be organised, and saying why they chose them and if they mean something to them.

Who said that ... ?

'We're more popular than Jesus Christ now.'
'Any colour, so long as it's black.'
'That's one small step for a man, one giant leap for mankind.'
'I have a dream today.'
'All I need to make a comedy is a park, a policeman and a pretty girl.'
'It's often safer to be in chains than to be free.'
'Ask not what your country can do for you; ask what you can do for your
    country.'
'I never forget a face, but I'll make an exception in your case.'
'Hell is other people.'
'I cannot believe that God plays dice with the Cosmos.'

Franz Kafka	Henry Ford	Groucho Marx
John Lennon	John F Kennedy	Martin Luther King
Neil Armstrong	Albert Einstein	Charlie Chaplin
Jean-Paul Sartre		

© Cambridge University Press 2000

KEY (in order): John Lennon, Henry Ford, Neil Armstrong, Martin Luther King, Charlie Chaplin, Franza Kafka, John F Kennedy, Groucho Marx, Jean-Paul Sartre, Albert Einstein.

2.47 Waving the flag

Summary: Country names and flags

Level: Elementary and above (Young learners)

Time: 1 hour (25 minutes on the Net)

Language: Country names, colours, shapes

Sites: http://www.photius.com/flags/flag_identifier.html

Notes: The Flag Identifier uses a novel interface where you start with a basic idea, i.e. vertical or horizontal stripes, etc., and keep making choices until you get to the picture of the flag you are looking for. For more flags, see: http://www.theodora.com/flags.html

Preparation

Draw the flag of the country you teach in and get students to identify it. Then draw the flag of the country you come from (if different). Draw enough flags to illustrate the main designs used (vertical stripes, horizontal stripes, solid colours). You may need to do some work on the important vocabulary: colours, horizontal, vertical, slanting, narrow, broad, stripe, star, cross, crest, above, below, in the centre, in the corner, etc. Elicit all the country names your students know. Do they know what the flags look like? Encourage them to draw the flags on the board (with coloured markers, perhaps) and describe them.

Online

You'll need to guide students through a first use of the webpage. If you choose Mexico, for example, and show them how to navigate through the interface: it's got vertical stripes (click on the link to the page with flags which have vertical stripes) ... 3 vertical stripes ... which are green and white and red, and there's a crest in the middle of the flag) and show them how to follow your description to get to the Mexican flag. Now let them choose 5 flags they like and play the description game with a partner.

Offline

Lots of towns and cities have flags too. Print out the blank flag templates at the site and have students design a flag for the town or city you work in. What is the town famous for, and how could this be represented on a flag? This activity can also be applied to a flag for the school, the class, or even individuals. Have a competition to judge the best flag produced.

Follow-ups / Variations

After going through the different designs flags can have, play a game where someone describes a flag, and the rest of the class have to find it. Use the page http://www.photius.com/flags/alphabetic_list.html which has small representations of all the flags.

You could also prepare a Find a flag which … game.

2.48 Dream houses

Summary: Students design their perfect house

Level: Advanced

Time: 90 minutes (50 minutes on the Net)

Language: Conditionals, housing vocabulary, descriptions

Sites: http://www.pathfinder.com/@@eyzHeAUAGCF17SaR/Life/dreamhouse/

Notes: This lesson is based around a website which has lots of graphics. It is a good idea to open the pages before a class visit.

Preparation

Start off the activity with the **Dream houses** discussion. Get some feedback on the discussion and try to establish common ground between all members of the class. You might like to do some preparatory revision work on language used for describing houses, prepositions, etc.

Online

The Life Magazine Dream House site has 'affordable' dream houses designed by top architects. Divide students up into groups and give each group a different house. Give them time to tour the house, looking at all the photos and descriptions. Then put groups together and get them to give each other a guided tour of their houses using the photos and their own descriptions. Here they must imagine they are estate agents and are desperate to sell the house they are showing. Repeat this until everyone has seen all the houses. Get feedback and discuss the merits of each house.

Offline

Print out the form from the Tell Us About Your Dream House section and give students a little time to think about it and fill it in. (Check the form as you may want to edit it before using it in class.) They then discuss it in pairs. If there is time, return to the Internet and fill in and send off the form online.

Follow-ups / Variations

This activity could be adapted for lower levels by simply using the pictures from the different houses. These pictures feature all kinds of rooms and furniture which can easily be exploited at all levels.

For higher levels, the Life site also features a link to a Design Your Dream Garden site.

Dream houses

If you had a lot of money and could design yourself a dream house, what would it be like? Think about the following sections, then compare in groups:

- house or apartment
- size, number and functions of rooms
- city centre, suburbs, countryside
- country or region
- exclusive area
- near to bus or train station
- space for entertaining
- space for working
- style of furniture and fittings
- extras: swimming pool, office, sauna, jacuzzi, air-conditioning, heating, etc.
- security
- privacy

© Cambridge University Press 2000

2.49 Net research ⊹

Summary: Using the Internet for basic research

Level: Mid-intermediate and above

Time: 1 hour (30 minutes on the Net)

Language: Synonyms, rhymes, doing and reporting on research

Sites: http://www.itools.com/research-it/

Notes: See also the translation pages at AltaVista
http://babelfish.altavista.com. For computing terminology see
http://www.pcwebopaedia.com/

Preparation

Give out the **Net research** activity and give students time to look through it
and fill in any answers they can.

Online

Take them to Research It! and show them the different sections, and how to
use them. This is an ideal opportunity to show students how to keep two
Internet browser windows open at the same time: one with the page they are
interested in, and another with a reference tool such as Research It! or the
translation page at AltaVista. This is easily achieved by opening Internet
Explorer or Netscape Communicator again and loading a different page.
You can then switch between them by clicking their respective buttons at the
bottom of your screen. Show them how to switch between windows, and also
how to use the *Back* button on the browser to return to the previous page.
This may have been covered earlier in a class on how to use the Internet.

Offline

Get feedback on the answers students have found and discuss their experiences in using the Net this way. Is it useful? Is it quicker or easier than using
traditional reference books? How do they feel about reading so much information on a computer screen for a comparatively long time?

Follow-ups / Variations

You may need to vary this activity to suit your students. All the answers to the activity below are easily available from the Research It! site.

If you teach students who speak one of the languages covered by the AltaVista translation service, show students how to use it as a bilingual dictionary while reading on the Net. Other translation options can be found at: http://www.logos.it

---

Net research

1 What is a scanner?
2 How many words do you know which rhyme with 'car'?
3 How many synonyms do you know for 'house'?
4 How do you say 'school' in Italian?
5 Can you think of an anagram for 'space'?
6 What does NATO stand for?
7 What is Volta famous for?
8 Who said 'All you need is love'?
9 What's the telephone code for Chicago in the USA?
10 How many Turkish lira can you get for US$25?

© Cambridge University Press 2000

2.50 What do you think of ...

Summary: Getting opinions

Level: Elementary and above

Time: 1 hour (20 minutes on the Net)

Language: Question forms, comparatives, superlatives

Sites: http://www.gigapoll.com/

Notes: The Giga Poll site is one of the many sites which allows you to create surveys and questionnaires which can be used online. No programming knowledge is necessary, and the interface is very easy to negotiate.

Preparation

Start off with the **What do you think of ...** questionnaire. This one has been devised for upper-intermediate students, so you might need to make the level higher or lower depending on the group you are going to do this activity with. This simple survey will give students ideas on the kind of questionnaires they might want to put together later.

Make sure students see the difference between the types of question in the survey (multiple choice and 'either / or'). Put them into groups of three or four and give them time to think about the things they think are important. (This can be anything from politics to entertainment to what's happening or available in their home town.) Encourage them to design questionnaires with different types of questions.

Online

Have them make their surveys on the website by filling in the forms and then get them to answer them themselves. Don't forget to make a note of the web addresses (URLs) assigned to the finished surveys once you have created them online. Now get students from other groups to try each other's surveys.

Offline

The survey addresses can be advertised on the school or institution notice-board and other classes invited to visit the computer facilities and vote. The surveys can also be printed and used offline in a speaking activity.

Follow-ups / Variations

Write to EFL listservs (see **Section 4**) and advertise your new surveys, inviting teachers and students to visit them and vote. Post results to the list at a later date. The surveys prepared in the **Online** part can, if printed, make the basis for a lively debate in class. This activity is easily adapted to very low levels where the subject can be food, drink, colours, animals, etc.

What do you think of ...

1 Who's the best actor?
   a) Brad Pitt   b) Pierce Brosnan   c) Keanu Reeves   d) Sean Connery

2 Who's the best singer?
   a) Madonna   b) Paul McCartney   c) Mick Jagger   d) Celine Dion

3 What would you do if you had $1 million to spare?
   a) Spend it   b) Save it   c) Give it to charity

4 What's the most expensive restaurant in town?
   a) ....   b) ....   c) ....   d) ....

5 How old are you?
   a) under 20   b) under 30   c) under 40   d) under 50   e) under 60

6 What sex are you?
   a) male   b) female

7 Do you like learning English?
   a) Yes   b) No

© Cambridge University Press 2000

2.51 Survival

Summary: Survival techniques and advice

Level: Upper-intermediate and above

Time: 1 hour (15 minutes on the Net)

Language: Advice, instructions, imperatives

Sites: http://www.survival-city.com/survival-city/surstratdisg.html

Notes: This site has other interesting sections on general survival.

Preparation

Survival City has lots of useful advice on how to survive diverse disasters such as earthquakes, flooding, hurricanes, landslides, fire, thunderstorms, tornadoes, volcanoes. Choose the ones you feel most appropriate and divide the class into groups, allocating a disaster to each group. Then have them brainstorm what to do in the event of the disaster, dividing the activity into before, during and after. Get feedback as a class.

Online

Give them time to look through their section, check what they thought of, and add to the advice from the information they find there.

Offline

As a class, go through the advice found on the different pages. Design a general 'preparing for a disaster' list with this information.

Follow-ups / Variations

The information gathered in the **Offline** stage could be turned into a colourful 'Warning!' poster, illustrated with pictures and practising some of the more usual structures found in this context: direct imperatives (Dos and Don'ts) advice and suggestions ('*Try to ...*', '*make sure you ...*', etc.).

Alternatively, try the **Survival** activity. This can be done as a simple discussion about priorities and uses. Are any of the items potentially more dangerous than helpful? Which items could be put to more than one use? A good example is the ball of string which could be used for making a raft (if wood was found) or for tying the overcoat up as a makeshift shelter.

Survival

Your ship is sinking next to a desert island. It is very hot and there is no shade or fresh water. You have time to grab 10 things from the boat. Decide which things you would take, and why:

A big sheet of plastic	10 boxes of matches
2 bottles of whisky	An overcoat
A torch	A gun with 20 bullets
A mirror	Sunglasses
A map	8 litres of water
A radio with batteries	A compass
A first-aid kit	A knife
A portable computer	2 chickens
A magnifying glass	An empty bottle
A ball of string	A spade

© Cambridge University Press 2000

2.52 Teen spirit

Summary: Talking about teenage life and issues

Level: Mid-intermediate and above

Time: 1 hour (30 minutes on the Net)

Language: Teenage problems

Sites: http://www.cyberteens.com/ http://www.ttt.org.il/
http://www.theteenzone.com/

Notes: This class is obviously aimed at teenage groups, but the theme of age and generation gaps can be exploited with older students too.

Preparation

Start with a general brainstorm of teenage issues – what are the most important issues and themes of teenage life? Some of the issues raised could include: music, parents, liberty, education, career, sexuality, going out, shopping, friends, etc. What are the main problems teenagers have?

Online

The websites in the notes to this activity are all produced by teenagers for teenagers. They are large, diverse sites, and as such are not ideally suited to planning an exact class. I have used them with the website review activity (see *Activity 2.55*) to engage students in a discussion of which sites might be useful for finding like-minded people. Alternatively, give students time to look through them and then have a class discussion about the interesting things they found while browsing.

CyberTeens has opportunities for students to submit stories, poems and artwork, as well as an interesting 'zine' (you will find 'zine' and 'e-zine' very common on the Net – they both refer to online amateur magazines); the Teen-to-Teen site has quizzes, games, a chat zone and regular public interest sections on world problems; the TeenZone has free email for teenagers, reviews, discussions and interviews.

If your students don't find anything useful in these sites, have them visit http://dir.yahoo.com/Society_and_Culture/Cultures_and_Groups/Teenagers/ This is the teenage section of Yahoo!

Offline

Discuss the sites found – which ones were interesting, which ones boring, etc. Have students write up a clean copy of the website review form (see the *FAQs* section) for later reference. This is an ideal opportunity to start a class website review file if you do not already keep one.

Follow-ups / Variations

There is plenty of opportunity here for a more wide-ranging discussion on the position of teenagers and adolescents in society. You might like to touch upon the subject of the clash between teenagers and adults, the different attitudes to teenage boys and girls in some societies, etc.

2.53 What's in a name?

Summary: Talking about people's names

Level: Lower-intermediate and above

Time: 75 minutes (40 minutes on the Net)

Language: Names and their meanings

Sites: http://www2.parentsoup.com/babynames/

Preparation

Start with the *Famous names* activity. Get feedback and discuss why people change their names? Are your students happy with theirs?

Online

Give out a list of all the names of people in the class. Give everyone a chance to find their name on the Meanings and Origins page of the Parent Soup page. Then do a walkround activity with everyone asking '*What's your name?*' and '*What does it mean?*' If some students don't find their name, encourage them to use Yahoo! or AltaVista for further searching.

Now ask students to think about what they would like their name to be if they were famous. They can used the Find It! page on the site to search for names by number of syllables, meaning, sex, letter of the alphabet, etc.

Encourage students to be adventurous and find themselves a new identity! The Famous Name page on this site can be used in this way too. Make sure they find out the significance of their new name too.

Offline

Now do a further walkround activity with students using their new identities and asking and answering the same questions as in the *Online* section (i.e. '*What's your name?*' and '*What does it mean?*').

Follow-ups / Variations

A good written follow-up would be for students to interview one of the new famous people and write up the interview.

Famous names

Can you match the original name of these famous people on the left with their 'stage' names on the right?

Bernard Schwartz	Sting
Rogers Nelson	Bono
Dino Paul Crocetti	Elton John
Frances Gumm	Marilyn Monroe
Marion Michael Morrison	John Wayne
George O'Dowd	George Michael
Eric Arthur Blair	Tony Curtis
Giogius Panayiotou	Dean Martin
Thomas Conner	Sean Connery
David Jones	David Bowie
Norma Jean Baker	Boy George
Paul Hewson	George Orwell
Reginald Dwight	Prince
Gordon Sumner	Judy Garland

© Cambridge University Press 2000

KEY: Bernard Schwartz – Tony Curtis; Rogers Nelson – Prince; Dino Paul Crocetti – Dean Martin; Frances Gumm – Judy Garland; Marion Michael Morrison – John Wayne; George O'Dowd – Boy George; Eric Arthur Blair – George Orwell; Giogius Panayiotou – George Michael; Thomas Conner – Sean Connery; David Jones – David Bowie; Norma Jean Baker – Marilyn Monroe; Paul Hewson – Bono; Reginald Dwight – Elton John; Gordon Sumner – Sting

2.54 Discoveries and inventions

Summary: Inventions which have changed our lives

Level: Upper-intermediate and above

Time: 1 hour (15 minutes on the Net)

Language: Passives, past tenses

Sites: http://www.invent.org/book/book-text/indexbyname.html

Notes: See also http://tqjunior.advanced.org/5847/homepage.htm and Yahoo!

Preparation

Brainstorm a list of inventions and discoveries which students think have changed people's lives. Try to get ten up on the board, then get students to put them in order of importance. Which ones could they live without, and which not? Now do the *Inventions and discoveries* activity.

Online

Divide the class into groups and take the inventions and discoveries which students thought were important and distribute them round the groups. Have students find out something more about the inventor or discoverer. Early finishers should be encouraged to 'wander' round the website looking at anyone else who interests them.

Offline

Students share what they have found out about the inventors and discoverers. Which one was the most prolific? Which the most important?

Follow-ups / Variations

For work on the passive in the *Preparation* stage, consider broadening the categories to take in paintings, buildings, discoveries, inventions, records, films, etc., thus allowing for a wider range of verbs (discover, invent, paint, direct, build, design).

125

A good follow-up activity is to talk about things which haven't been invented yet. Have students make a list of things which have been talked about, but not yet built, e.g. flying cars, teleportation, space colonies, etc. What would they like to live to see? What do they think are going to be the most important advances over the coming years?

Work on writing biographies of famous inventors and discoverers can also make a good follow-up activity. See the Biographical Dictionary at http://www.s9.com/biography/

Inventions and discoveries

Can you match the person with their invention or discovery?

Alfred Nobel	Kodak camera
Alexander Graham Bell	Light bulb
Alexander Fleming	Dynamite
George Eastman	Elevator
John Logie Baird	Radio
Thomas Edison	Telephone
Guglielmo Marconi	Television
Chester Carlson	Penicillin
Elisha Otis	Photocopier

Do you know when these things were invented/discovered?
Which of these do you think are important?
Which of them could you do without?

© Cambridge University Press 2000

KEY: Alfred Nobel – Dynamite, 1867; Alexander Graham Bell – Telephone, 1876; Alexander Fleming – Penicillin, 1928; George Eastman – Kodak camera, 1888; John Logie Baird – Television, 1926; Thomas Edison – Light bulb, 1879; Guglielmo Marconi – Radio, 1895; Chester Carlson – Photocopier, 1938; Elisha Otis – Elevator, 1853

2.55 Reviewing a website

Summary: Reviewing and classifying websites

Level: Elementary and above

Time: 1 hour (40 minutes on the Net)

Language: Adjectives, language used for reviewing

Sites: No specific sites

Notes: If you use the Net regularly with classes, you will want to keep a record of popular and successful websites. This activity encourages students to do the same.

Preparation

Have a group discussion about good websites students have visited. Get some addresses and talk about what made them good: was it the content, the presentation, or something else? Build up a set of criteria for reviewing websites. This can be done by simply taking students' ideas or by using the website review form (see the *FAQs* section). Note that the website review form is designed for teacher use, so it will need some adaptation. You will also need to find examples of websites for later review – use ones from your own surfing experience – for use in the *Online* section.

Online

Put students in small groups and get each member in turn to give the other members of the group a quick tour of a website they like, pointing out the best features and explaining why it is good. Remind students at this point how to *Bookmark* or add a site to the *Favorites*. Now give out blank review forms and ask students to visit one or two sites and review them. Make sure they know that the forms they fill in must make sense to other people reading them later.

Offline

Share the newly-created reviews around the class, discussing the websites visited. Establish a class folder for website information and decide together how to classify the website review forms. It's a good idea to appoint someone to look after the folder and make sure it is up-to-date. This will, over time, become an invaluable resource for the whole class.

3   Projects

One of the wonderful features of the Internet is that anyone with a little common sense and time can contribute to it. In this section we'll be taking a look at how you and your students can get involved. The first couple of projects revolve around email exchanges and student discussion lists. Later projects are based on webpages and sites which you can make with your students.

3.0 Email penpal exchanges

Once you are familiar with email, you might like to explore the possibility of opening out its use to your students. One of the best ways of doing this is by organising an email penpal exchange with other students in another country. This is immensely motivating for students, as the combination of technology, speed of communication and writing for a 'real' audience combine to provide the sort of experience which is difficult to create in the classroom alone.

Starting off

Before entering into any commitment to do a penpal exchange, you'll find it necessary to spend some time teaching your students how to use computers, how to write, send and receive email, etc. It is not advisable to try to teach these basic skills at the same time as you ask them to write to their partners. Spending some time on basic computer use and Internet skills before starting the exchange will help you avoid problems once it is under way. (For more help on introducing your students to computers, see the first visit lesson plans in *Section 2*.) When you have done the groundwork, it's time to think about how to get an exchange going.

There are plenty of EFL sites on the Net which have penpal pages, and it's a good idea to have a look at these sites first, just to get some idea of what people are doing. One nice penpal site is at its-online (http://its-online.com)

where students can leave messages and answer messages left by other would-be writers. To introduce the activity:

a. Give students a chance to browse the penpals of the month
b. Give them the *Electronic penpals* activity and let them find the answers
c. Get feedback and ask students which two people they've decided to write to
d. Spend some time working on a good introductory message
e. Send the messages

Electronic penpals

Find someone ...

1) from the same country as you...
2) from a country you'd like to visit...
3) the same age and sex as you..
4) with similar interests to you...

Find someone who ...

1) wouldn't like to hear from you! ....
2) likes something you've never heard of....................................
3) does something you'd like to do..
4) likes a group you like. ....

Find ...

1) an Internet word for 'email penpal'..
2) a spelling mistake you can correct. ....
3) someone you definitely wouldn't write to. ....
4) two people you'd love to write to. ....

This can be a very stimulating exercise and excellent practice for most students. There is, however, a down side. Many individuals put penpal messages on more than one site. Often they get too many messages and decide not to bother replying, or they decide on one person who really interests them and ignore the rest. It can be a very disheartening experience to excitedly check your mail every day, waiting for a response and never getting one, so it is best to warn students in advance that there are no guarantees.

> **TIP** ☑
>
> You can get more advice on how to find penpals and how to set up an email exchange at the website which accompanies this book. Visit the website at http://www.cambridge.org/elt/chlt/internet and look for the email section.

Finding partners

If its-online doesn't have the sort of people you are looking for, there are plenty of other penpal sites including the Student Email Connection at Dave Sperling's ESL Cafe (http://www.eslcafe.com) and at NetPals, which is part of the Internet for Learning educational site http://www.rmplc.co.uk/meeting/penpals.html For more addresses, see the *FAQs* section at the end of the book.

The best penpal exchanges work class-to-class. And the best way to find a class with which to exchange is to advertise on one of the email mailing lists (listservs) such as TESL-L or NETEACH-L (see *Section 4* and the *FAQs* section).

Guidelines

Where I work in Barcelona, Spain we have had very successful exchanges for the last two years with a school in the US. Their students are studying Spanish, so we have been running a bilingual exchange: our students write 70% English and 30% Spanish, their US counterparts do the opposite. This has helped both groups immensely, as it gives them a chance to really express themselves – at least for part of each letter – and often to include the type of language we as teachers tend not to cover in the classroom.

A good exchange will depend on many factors. Here are some considerations:

1) Find a teacher in your partner school who understands the technology and is committed to the exchange.

2) Match each student up with two or more in the partner school. This means that if people leave, or are absent for a while, each student will have at least one person to write to.

3) Give students access to individual email accounts. If the place where you teach does not have the resources for this, try using one of the free web-based email services such as Hotmail http://www.hotmail.com For more information, see the website list in the *FAQs* section of this book. Bear in

mind, however, that free web-based email services are often very slow, especially when accessed from Europe.

4) Prepare your students carefully. Point out that email still takes time to arrive, that some people write more quickly, and reply sooner than others. Be prepared for the occasions when some students don't have a letter to reply to.

5) Point out that cultural differences are important, and that allowances must be made when writing to people abroad. We once had an unfortunate incident with the translation of a Spanish swear word which is inoffensive in Spanish, yet rather stronger in English. These matters should be dealt with as they arise.

6) Try to establish a program of message content, while not disturbing your students' natural desire to communicate. I have found that a simple task for each letter (e.g. describe a typical school day in your country, a typical day at work, etc.) helps to give focus to the writing. Each message can be divided into carrying out the task, and a section for whatever the student wants to write about.

With some careful planning, and a good partner school, you can easily set up and run a very successful exchange. Here are notes on a couple of example exchanges (between two countries) with which I have been involved in the last couple of years:

Sample exchange 1

This exchange was between a school of English in Spain and a secondary school in Milton Keynes, UK where the students study Spanish. Initially, two classes of twelve students between 13 and 15 years old were paired up and the exchange, which started in October, had the following program:

- Students in both countries sent off a brief description of themselves in both languages (Spanish and English). The messages were designed to look more or less like a typical penfriend advert in a magazine.
- Students were then allocated two partners in the other country, bearing in mind any preferences wherever possible.
- One set of students made the first contact with a letter of introduction and details of Christmas in their country. The other students replied before the Christmas holidays with a similar message.
- From January onwards, students were encouraged to make contact at least once a month, with the teachers suggesting possible topics for inclusion in their messages. They were encouraged to write about the topic and then move on to whatever personal content they wanted to include.

Sample exchange 2

This exchange was with the same school as exchange 1, but for higher level students in both schools. The project concentrated on items of news and social topics with the following program:

- On the first school day of every month, the teachers decided together on a topic of world interest, and separately on a topic of national interest.
- By the 10th of each month, the students sent off any information they had gathered (usually from the Internet and local sources of news) related to these two topics. This information was sent in the students' own language, and they undertook to provide vocabulary glossaries and explanations where necessary.
- During the following ten days the material received was used in class by the teachers, and students compared reactions in both countries to the item of world news, as well as learning what was important to their partners on a national scale.
- In the final third of the month, students sent and received messages in which they talked about their reactions to the news items and had the opportunity to ask follow-up questions, as well as 'socialise'.

Note: At the end of each month the students got together on IRC (Internet Relay Chat – a live text-based chat system) to 'talk' to each other in a group debate. See **Section 4 Advanced Net** for more information about using IRC. These sessions were saved to disk and used as follow-up material later.

VARIATIONS: A TIME CAPSULE

An interesting add-on to a penpal exchange is to arrange for you and your partner school to exchange 'Time Capsules' – boxes (either real and full of real objects, or 'virtual', with scanned images, brochures, etc.) of information and realia from your country or area. This can become quite a large project, with groups of students working on different aspects of life in the area, and is a great way to stimulate interest from both groups.

Email exchange tips

1. Don't underestimate the time students will want to spend on writing their messages. You might be surprised at how much more effort they put into writing to their partners than they usually do when writing for you. Don't take it to heart – it is usually much more exciting for them than a more traditional writing exercise!

2. If you are short of time in the classroom and don't want to (or can't) spend a whole lesson writing messages, have students write them at home and look over them at the beginning of the next class. Students with computers at home can even type the messages and bring them in on disk, thus saving even more time.

3. Remember, this is not an exam composition, so there is probably no need to insist on total accuracy. Besides anything else, too much correction may inhibit students' desire to communicate and take the fun out of the project.

4. As with accuracy, insisting on the content of messages will not allow your students to really establish a relationship with the people they are writing to. I've found that breaking the message exchange down into two components – task (a set topic students have to write about first) and free writing – gives some focus to each assignment while allowing everyone time and space to express themselves.

5. As you saw in *Section 1*, email messages are usually written in a very informal way so don't insist on your students writing 'model' compositions during an email exchange.

3.1 Writing projects

Getting students published

There are plenty of opportunities for your students to publish their writing on the Net. Not only does this give them an immense feeling of satisfaction and pride in their work, but it also encourages them to take more time over presentation, accuracy, etc. One such place is the student magazine called WriteNow! at http://www.ihes.com/Sresource Published on an occasional basis, this magazine has all the features of a normal publication: from sports and arts to science and technology and international news. There's even a section for really young learners, who can send drawings and cartoon stories to be published.

All this can be done by having students prepare and type up their articles, then mail them to the submission address found at the website. There's no limit as to what you can send, so it's another ideal opportunity for doing an extended project. The great difference here is that the final audience for the project work is enormous. Other addresses for submitting student writing can be found in the *FAQs* section.

TIP ☑

There is often a lot of discussion and disagreement about the 'ethical' aspects of putting student work on the Net, with regard to copyright and the publication of information about students.

Most people agree that it is sensible to have students (or their parents or legal guardians) sign a release form – giving the school or institution permission to publish student writing – before publishing their work. A sample release form is provided as a guideline in the *FAQs* section. It will probably need adapting for your purposes and place of work.

3.2 Web-based projects

It is beyond the scope of this book to teach teachers how to make complicated webpages, but the examples in this section are all very easy and straightforward. You will find these sample projects and advice on how to write webpages at the website which accompanies the book, at http://www.cambridge.org/elt/chlt/internet

While you can immediately make use of the email based projects, it would be advisable to visit the website and have a good look at the examples before attempting to put together a webpage with your students. (See the *FAQs* section of this book for more information about websites which help with making webpages.)

If all else fails, most modern word processing software such as Microsoft Word has an option to save documents as HTML (HyperText Mark-Up Language) – the language used to make webpages – files, so if you can word process, you can easily make a webpage these days. Another option is to use the editor which is built into Netscape.

Getting students involved in actually producing webpages and putting them up on the Net is a wonderful way of letting them share their thoughts, culture and customs with other people round the world. Obviously, projects such as these work best if there is some kind of collaboration between countries, but simple pages which allow for feedback from the person visiting them will work well too.

The activities in this section vary in length from a simple class, to an extended project over a considerable amount of time. Most of them can be made very easily using the HTML possibilities of any modern word processor or text editor. Where extra software or skills are necessary, you will find pointers to relevant resources.

There are templates (a template is a rough model for a webpage, and contains common elements, titles and pictures, etc., which can be used as starting points for making websites) and example files for most of these projects on the book website at http://www.cambridge.org/elt/chlt/internet

---

TIP ☑

It is potentially dangerous to publish personal information about people on the Internet. This is particularly true when working with children and young learners. Publishing names, addresses, contact information and photographs of such groups of people should be done with great care (if at all) and with permission of a parent or legal guardian. When in doubt, it is better to err on the side of caution.

It would be good idea to start with the templates and work with them for a while. They have been kept deliberately simple to understand and adapt and in most cases will be more than enough to get any project up-and-running. But before you get started, here are the basic skills you will need to produce a small website:

A simple webpage is a text file which has a few instructions for formatting text (e.g. making it **bold** or *italic*), adding images and linking to other pages. These instructions are called HTML tags. Most HTML tags are made up of two parts: an opening tag (e.g. <B> = turn bold text on) and a closing tag (</B> = turn bold text off).

You can write webpages using any word processing program or text editor. For the purposes of this book, I will be using the Windows text editor Notepad. This is perhaps not the best overall tool, but rather one guaranteed to be on most computers these days, and also very simple to use.

There are also plenty of expensive programs (in the region of $200 – $300) for making webpages. Rather than typing out the HTML tags yourself, you put together the various elements of the webpage by adding pictures and text as you would with a good word processor – you can then select text and change fonts, colours, sizes, etc., with the click of a button. The advantage of these tools is that they make webpage design more like word processing, something with which most teachers are familiar these days. The other advantage to these editors is that you can see exactly what the webpage will look like as you make it, without having to constantly look at it in a web browser.

Two of the best are: Dreamweaver from Macromedia (http://www.macromedia.com) and FrontPage Express from Microsoft (http://www.microsoft.com) – they both work very much like a word processor, but are quite complicated to learn. Free programs which take some of the hard work out of making webpages can be found on the Internet at the TUCOWS site (http://www.tucows.com) and of these I would recommend Arachnophilia.

TIP ☑

You can start making webpages with the Page Composer that comes
with Netscape Communicator, or with FrontPage Express that is
included in the Microsoft Internet Explorer. By doing this you'll never
have to come into contact with HTML. However, if you can't understand
HTML you'll never really understand how a webpage is made, or why it
isn't working if something goes wrong.

Basic HTML

When you look at a webpage in a web browser like Netscape Communicator
or Internet Explorer you don't normally see the HTML tags because the
browser interprets them as instructions:

HTML text file   *Browser view*

My name is <B>Gavin Dudeney</B>.   My name is **Gavin Dudeney**.

The HTML tag (or instruction) you can see in the example: <B> tells the
browser to make the following text bold. When you want the text to stop
being bold, we put </B> (the '/' character means 'stop' or 'end').

So, to make a webpage you use a text editor to write the content and the
tags which will format it. To view a webpage you use a browser.

TIP ☑

You can have more than one program running on your computer at the
same time. While you are making webpages, it is a good idea to have
your text editor and a web browser running. As you make changes, you
can see them in your browser.

Below is the basic framework of a webpage. Try running Notepad (or
similar) and typing in these tags:

```
<HTML>
<HEAD>
<TITLE>My first webpage</TITLE>
</HEAD>
```

```
<BODY>
Welcome to my first webpage
</BODY>
</HTML>
```

Now click on *File* and choose *Save As* and call it '*page1.htm*' then click on the *Save* button, making sure you know where you are saving it on your hard disk. Your Notepad window should look like this:

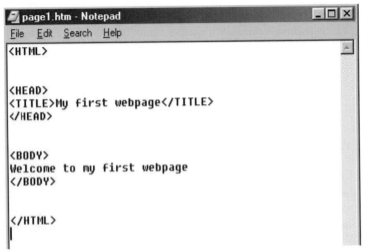

Open up this new webpage in your web browser. In Internet Explorer, click on *File* go to *Open* and choose *Browse* and explore your hard disk until you get to your new webpage. Double click on the file name and then click on *OK*. In Netscape Communicator, click on *File* select *Open Page* and go to *Choose File* and explore your hard disk until you get to your new webpage. Double click on the file name and then click on *Open*. In Internet Explorer your page should look like this:

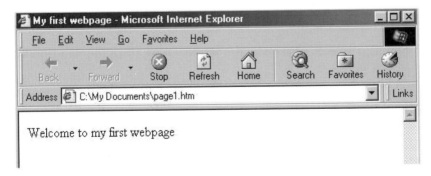

If you've got this far, congratulations – you've made your first webpage! Now let's look at what all those tags mean.

HTML tags	What they do
<HTML>	tells the browser this is the start of a webpage
<HEAD>	the head holds important information
<TITLE>My first webpage</TITLE>	the title is displayed at the top of the browser
</HEAD>	the end of the head
<BODY>	the body holds the content of a webpage
Welcome to my first webpage	some plain text displayed on the page
</BODY>	the end of the body
</HTML>	tells the browser this is the end of the webpage

Go back to your Notepad document and change the text '*Welcome to my first webpage*' to '*Here's some different text*'. Save the changes by clicking on *File* and then *Save*. Now click on your browser window and click the *Refresh* button (Netscape users click on *Reload*). You should see the changes displayed instantly.

HANDS ON 🖘

Try changing the title of your page. Don't forget to save any changes you make to your HTML page before trying to look at it in your browser.

Now that you know how to make, save and view a page you can move on to adding other features to it.

Adding an image to a webpage

You put an image on a webpage by using the IMG tag. Images must be either JPG or GIF files. GIFs are usually logos and drawings using a maximum of

256 colours, while JPGs are for high-quality photographs. You can find plenty of free images to use on your webpages by searching the Internet. Here's how the IMG tag works:

HTML text file   *Browser view*

<IMG SRC="arrow.gif">   →

HANDS ON 🖾

Use AltaVista to search for free web graphics. When you find pictures you think you might want to use, save them in the same place as your webpage. **Make sure that you are free to use images before saving them and adding them to your pages.**

To save an image from a webpage right click on it with the mouse button and choose the *Save Image As ...* option.

Changing text colours and formatting

You can make text bold, italicised or underline it, as well as using colours to enhance the look of your page. Try using these tags in your sample page:

HTML text file	*Browser view/effect*
My name is <B>Gavin Dudeney</B>.	My name is **Gavin Dudeney**.
I live in <I>Spain</I>	I live in *Spain*
I am an <U>English teacher</U>	I am an <u>English teacher</u>
My car is <FONT COLOR="Green">green</FONT>	My car is green
My jacket is <FONT COLOR="Blue">blue</FONT>	My jacket is blue
I hate <FONT COLOR="Red">red<"/FONT"> pens	I hate red pens
This is <FONT SIZE="7">important</FONT>	This is important
This is <FONT SIZE="4">quite important</FONT>	This is quite important
<CENTER>this text is centred</CENTER>	this text is centred
 	puts an empty line on the page
<P>	starts a new paragraph

TIP

When you find a webpage you like on the Net, you can see how it has been made by clicking on *View* and going to *Source* (in Netscape try *View* then *Document Source*). This will show you the HTML for the page. You can then copy the parts you like for your own pages.

Changing document colours

You can decide on a background colour for your page and default colours for your text and links by changing the body definition for your website:

HTML text file	Browser effect
<BODY BGCOLOR="Yellow">	changes the background of the page to yellow
<BODY BGCOLOR="Red" TEXT="White">	the background changes to red and normal text is displayed white
<BODY TEXT="White" link="Red">	a white text with red hyperlinks

HANDS ON

Go back to the sample page you made earlier and add some more text. Change the colour and style of different pieces of text. Don't forget to save the file before refreshing the view in your browser.

Adding hypertext links

You can link text and images on your page to:

• other pages you have made;
• other websites;
• your email address so that people can contact you.

When someone clicks on one of these links, they will be taken to the new page, site or to their email program:

HTML *text file*	Browser *view/effect*
<A HREF="page2.htm">on to page 2</A>	on to page 2 when someone clicks on the link it opens another webpage called page2.htm
<A HREF="http://www.cnn.com">visit CNN</A>	visit CNN when someone clicks on the link they are taken to the CNN website
<A HREF="mailto:me@mail.com">send me email</A>	send me email when someone clicks the link, their email program opens with a new message to me

When you have finished making a website, you need to put it onto the Internet for others to see. The easiest way of doing this is to use one of the free services for publishing websites on the Internet. There are many companies and websites which offer this service, and you could start by visiting one of the following:

Geocities (http://www.geocities.com)
Tripod (http://www.tripod.com)
Angelfire (http://www.angelfire.com)
Xoom (http://www.xoom.com)

Webpage making tips

1. Make sure you save all your files and images in the same place (directory or folder) on your hard disk. By doing this you can be sure that all the links you have made – and all the images you have added – will work properly.
2. Give your pages short, easily recalled names so that they can be easily identified, remembered and retrieved (ones with long difficult names often don't work!).
3. Don't use capital letters in file names: they will work properly in Windows, but may not work on the Internet.

4. Plan your website on paper before you start making it. When you have a good structure, make a template and use it to make all the pages you need. Your template should be a simple 'model' page for your site, with all the common elements in it (navigation links, titles, etc.) – you can then copy this file each time you want to make a new page.

5. Spellcheck, proofread and test your site well before you make it available to the rest of the world. During testing, make sure all the links work properly, all the images display correctly and it looks how you expected it to look. For an example of a simple student website, see *Sample projects–Example: Our Class*.

When you have experimented with the basic guide to making webpages and have put some pages on the Internet, you'll be ready to start working on the projects in this section. If you find that you want to learn more about making webpages, check the links in the *FAQs* section at the back of the book. Now let's move on to some sample projects.

TIP ☑

Don't forget that you can find sample templates (model pages) for these projects at the website which goes with this book. The templates are designed for easy editing from within a simple HTML editor like the Netscape Page Composer. Visit http://www.cambridge.org/elt/chlt/internet for more information.

Sample projects

Listed here are ten basic ideas for sample projects which lend themselves well to the medium of the webpage. They are just suggestions, and you should adapt the themes, content and site structure to suit your students.

LOCAL FOOD

This project aims to give people around the world the opportunity of getting to know the food of a particular country. The webpage might contain photographs of various dishes, sample menus from restaurants, a look at local ingredients, foodstuffs and wines. There is a mail link or small form for visitors to fill in. No recipes are given on the pages, but visitors are invited to write in and request recipes they're interested in. In a mixed nationality group, focus on national dishes.

FESTIVALS

In this webpage project, students prepare descriptions of local festivals which happen throughout the year. This is a good example of an ongoing project. Every time a new festival comes along, students add it to their festival pages – descriptions, photographs, perhaps even sound or video. The photographs can be personal ones of the students and their families and friends involved in the various celebrations. Links to external resources can also be added.

Visitors are invited to write in with descriptions of festivals in their country or region, or simply to ask for more information on any of the festivals on the website itself. Again, for a mixed nationality class this can simply be made into a look at the most important festival in each country represented.

TIP ☑

Business students can benefit enormously from a webpage project. They can look at large company websites before going on to make a website for their company or business. Remember, most commerce on the Net is done in English, so this is an ideal opportunity for making a bilingual website. See the *FAQs* section for some good business sites.

IN THE NEWS

This project takes a look at local or national issues. Students make a mock-up of a newspaper featuring issues which are important in their country at the time of writing. This particular website invites questions and reactions from visitors and includes a 'write to the editor' page. For a collaborative project, try finding a school in another country and doing an international edition of the newspaper.

For mixed nationality classes, the newspaper can be modified to resemble a typical magazine which collects stories from round the world.

TIP ☑

You can find schools in other countries who are interested in email exchanges and collaborative projects by joining educational listservs and mailing lists (see *Section 4*).

Getting involved in a collaborative project is usually more rewarding for students since they have an immediate audience for their work. Added to this, a joint project provides plenty of opportunity for communication.

SQUARE EYES

What's the TV like where you live? This webpage focuses both on content and programming, and takes a look at personal preferences and viewing habits. Students provide a summary of a typical day's viewing where they live, coupled with their views on TV and a summary of their viewing habits. Visitors are invited to write in to discuss programs they have in common, talk about their viewing habits, ask about the quality of TV, etc.

WHAT'S THE STORY?

Students choose popular traditional stories from their country and put them up on the Web. If possible accompany these stories by drawings, information about the writers, the setting, and perhaps some historical or geographical background. The stories can be left unfinished, and visitors are invited to write in suggesting possible endings. These are posted up and voted on before the real endings are revealed.

THE BIG ISSUE

This website looks at an issue of local or national interest. The issue is explored in depth, considering the pros and cons and looking at possible solutions. You may decide that polemic issues such as abortion, drugs, divorce, are more important than say, whether the local government should provide more parking spaces in the city, but it is often the smaller issues which fascinate people from other countries.

Encourage students to link their pages to other resources on the Net which feature similar information. Finally, add an email link or simple form for visitors to give their reactions and suggestions, etc.

OUR CLASS

This is a big project looking at the entire class: the individuals, the teacher, activities in class, hobbies and interests outside class, the city or town, and the region. This website includes a photo of the class; clicking on a student takes the visitor to his/her page with personal information and a mail link. Visitors to the site are encouraged to write to the students and ask them questions about themselves. A variation of this project is one which focuses on the town or country.

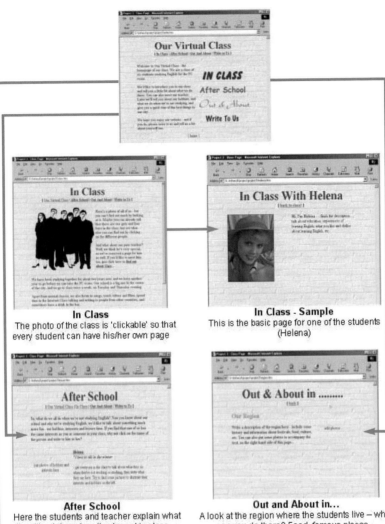

In Class
The photo of the class is 'clickable' so that every student can have his/her own page

In Class - Sample
This is the basic page for one of the students (Helena)

After School
Here the students and teacher explain what they like doing when they're not in class

Out and About in...
A look at the region where the students live – what can you do there? Food, famous places...

Out and About in...
A look at the town where the students live

This is a simple project which you will find at the website. Students work in groups to produce different sections, but also have the opportunity to express themselves individually on their personal page. The Write to Us link allows visitors to write and ask questions, leave comments, etc.

THE BIG SCREEN

What are the big films of the moment? What sort of films do students prefer, and who are their favourite actors and actresses? This website includes film reviews, statistics on cinema going habits, biographies of actors and actresses (with photos) and information on local stars. Visitors are invited to contribute with film reviews and opinions on film stars. The site could also include links to good film sites such as Hollywood.Com (http://www.hollywood.com) and the Internet Movie Database (http://www.imdb.com).

LOCAL HEROES

Who are the famous people in the students' country – the national heroes? This website has a gallery of famous people. Visitors can visit different pages and find out about them all reading biographies and looking at photos, etc., including views by the students on which ones have been most influential and why. There is an email link for visitors to write in and give information about the heroes from their countries which are then added to the 'And Also ...' page. In multi-cultural classes, each nationality represented can make a page about a hero from their country.

JUST FOR LAUGHS

What do people find funny? This website has views and opinions on humour, a questionnaire to find out people's attitudes and a section for jokes and funny stories. This would be an ideal opportunity for students to draw illustrations for the jokes and stories and add them to the webpage. Visitors are asked to give their opinions on what is and isn't funny, and to send in a joke or story from their country.

TIP ☑

When you have finished a website and put it on the Internet, don't forget to visit the major search engines to submit a link to your new site. If it works, you'll get more visitors and more feedback. You'll find links on the front pages of most search engines: look for options such as *Submit a URL* or *Add a page*. Follow the link and fill in the form you find there. If everything works properly, your page will be added to the database.

Write to student and teacher mailing lists (see **Section 4**) to encourage people to visit your site.

These are just a few examples of useful class projects. These can be done both as stand-alone projects in a class, or as collaborative projects with other schools and students around the world. The secret is to get students writing and producing for the Internet, and to give them the opportunity to work with other people and/or get interaction from the end-user of their work.

Project Tips

1. Don't aim to produce anything which is beyond your own technical ability – fit the content to your skills to avoid problems during the production process.
2. Remember that the computer skills and time necessary to produce a finished product should not be so demanding as to detract from the language production. If students spend more time on – and have greater problems with – the technical aspects of a project, they will not benefit linguistically.
3. If collaborating on a project, fix a timetable of deadlines and responsibilities and make sure everyone sticks to them. It can be very frustrating for students to have to wait for a lazy partner.
4. Allow students to do as much of the decisionmaking and production as they can. This gives them a greater sense of ownership and responsibility for the project.

TIP ☑

If you don't have access to a lot of material for a particular project which interests your students, use the search skills you learnt in *Section 1* to find the material on the Internet. Remember to check the copyright of anything you decide to use. For more information, see The Copyright Website which can be found at http://www.benedict.com or the numerous articles and opinions at the Electronic Freedom Foundation's site at http://www.eff.org

---

4   Advanced Net

Section 4 of the book introduces the reader to some more advanced uses of the Internet in teaching: multimedia, listservs, browser caching, online chat.

There are hundreds of different ways of communicating by means of an Internet connection, and as you gain more experience you may want to branch out and try different things. And when you do feel the need to extend your knowledge or experience, you can use the search skills you have acquired in this book to find help and information to get you started. That really is the strong point of the Internet: once you know the basics, you can use the Net itself to learn the rest.

Having said this, however, I would like to offer some suggestions as to what you could do next – both in terms of enhancing your online experiences and also of making it easier for you to communicate with other teachers and find what you are looking for.

4.0 Browser enhancements

Today's modern browser includes software for viewing websites, reading newsgroups, sending and receiving email and much more. It can easily cope with pictures, text and simple sound. However, to get the most out of the Web you will need to add a few little extras to Netscape Communicator or Internet Explorer.

These extras are called plug-ins, and are basically small programs that extend the capability of your browser in a specific way, giving you, for example, the ability to show multimedia presentations and animations, hear live sound and watch live video or play games and do activities. These plug-ins are developed at a phenomenal rate, and can be obtained free from the Netscape (http://www.netscape.com) and Explorer (http://www.microsoft.com) homepages.

It's worth noting that if you have installed Internet Explorer 4 (or above) or Netscape Communicator 4 (or above) then your browser will already be equipped with most of the more useful plug-ins such as Shockwave Flash Player and Real Audio and you will only have to install additional ones (e.g. the Acrobat Reader, Director Shockwave) as the need arises.

Each time that you visit a website which requires a plug-in, your browser will first check to see if you have it installed. If you do, the page will work normally. If you don't have that particular plug-in, you will be asked if you want to get it and have it installed. You must decide if you want it or not. Once it's installed to work with your browser, every time you visit a page which requires this plug-in you will have instant access to the information there.

TIP ☑

Plug-ins can slow down your browser quite considerably, and fill up your hard disk. Make sure that you are really going to need a plug-in in the future before installing it on your system.

My experience would suggest that there are really only a handful of truly useful plug-ins. The best three are listed below. With these plug-ins, your browser will be fully equipped to cope with most websites.

Real Audio (also known as Real Player)

Real Audio allows your browser to reproduce audio and video, both pre-recorded and live. This can vary in content from simple recorded sound files of the type found at the BBC World Service website (http://www.bbc.co.uk) and video clips (see the Hollywood.com site at http://www.hollywood.com), to 24-hour live TV as shown at the Fox News site (http://www.foxnews.com) and live radio (try BBC Radio 5 Live at http://www.bbc.co.uk/radio5/live/live.html). The best place to get the plug-in, or the more sophisticated Real Player is at the Real site http://www.real.com

Shockwave

Get Shocked! Shock your browser! If you come across these words, or similar, when you're browsing a website, they mean that somewhere in the site you are looking at there is a 'shocked' presentation. Shockwave, from Macromedia (http://www.macromedia.com) allows you to visualise animations, hear sounds, watch videos, try multiple choice quizzes, games and puzzles and enjoy activities which allow for interaction between you and the website. More and more pages are using Shockwave or a similar presentation software called Flash these days – visit the Macromedia site to get the plug-in.

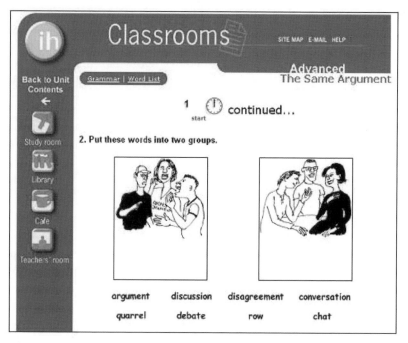

Students can click and drag the vocabulary into the two picture categories. When they have finished, they get feedback.

Adobe Acrobat

Adobe Acrobat files (often also known as PDF files) are complex documents which require more formatting and advanced presentation than a simple webpage allows. Many national newspapers which publish on the Web use this format so that viewers can see the newspaper almost as the real thing would look if you bought it at the newsagents. The Adobe Acrobat Reader plug-in can be found at http://www.adobe.com

4.1 Talking to other teachers – mailing lists

Perhaps the easiest way to get something out of the Net is to learn from other people with more experience than yourself. Language teachers as a group were quick to realise the potential of the Net in their field of work, and have been working with it for over 10 years. One excellent result of this long-term experience is that there are many thousands of teachers who are constantly in touch with each other, and sharing their experiences and resources with each other. The easiest way into this new world is to join a listserv.

Listservs are electronic mailing lists for specialist subjects. They are basically a collection of people interested in a particular subject or hobby who communicate with each other by email on a daily basis. All this communication is handled by a computer program which takes care of subscriptions, distributing the messages to subscribers and archiving past themes and discussions for future reference.

TESL-L

The most famous EFL related listserv is TESL-L (it stands for Teachers of English as a Second Language Listserv) and you can find it at listserv@cunyvm.cuny.edu It's based on a computer at the City University of New York in the United States. This educational listserv has been running for many years, and has well over 20,000 members.

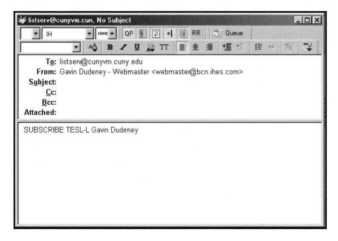

You join a listserv by sending an email message to a computer – you can see how to do this in the illustration above. When you send your subscription message to the listserv, remember that you're sending a message to a computer, and not to a person. Make sure that you put no information other than that which is required. If your subscription is successful you will receive a confirmation within a short period of time. This confirmation message is very important – not only does it give you information about how the listserv works, but it also tells you what you can and can't do on the list. Read it carefully before you start to use the list.

> **TIP** ☑
>
> Listservs can generate a lot of messages on a daily basis if they are very popular. Don't subscribe to too many at the same time or you'll be overloaded with mail. If you find you do need to unsubscribe, send a message to the listserv as you did when you subscribed, changing the word 'subscribe' for 'unsubscribe'.

NETEACH-L

Another useful listserv is NETEACH-L (listserv@raven.cc.ukans.edu) which is located on a computer in Kansas. NETEACH-L is a listserv for teachers who use (or would like to use) the Internet in their teaching. It has over 10,000 subscribers and is a great place to start finding out how teachers are using Internet resources in their classes. Despite its name, you'll find that participants discuss all issues of CALL and technology in the classroom.

NETEACH-L works in the same way as TESL-L, the only difference being that no-one vets the messages – when you send one to the list it is automatically sent out to all the subscribers. This means that you have to think a little more carefully before sending the message in the first place, and make sure that you want all those people to see what you are writing, and that it's suitable for the list. For more information on NETEACH-L, visit http://thecity.sfsu.edu/~funweb/neteach.htm .

These are just two of a list of thousands of listservs on many different subjects. For a full list of lists, visit Liszt at http://www.liszt.com/ where you will find an exhaustive database of Internet lists covering over 80,000 different fields including most major world languages.

Advantages of listservs

As far as language teachers are concerned, there really are a lot of benefits to be had from joining a listserv. Most of us have limited access to other teachers, teacher trainers, material and ideas, wherever we work. Joining a listserv effectively places us in the biggest 'teachers' room' in the world, with thousands of colleagues to talk to all the time.

A good reason for joining TESL-L specifically is that they have an enormous archive of past discussions and teacher resource files around various subjects built up over the years. These can be requested and received by email too, by using the *archive* facility.

TESL-L is also occasionally used as a medium for teaching. A couple of years ago it was possible to follow a course in Fluency First entirely taught by email. People who decided to do the course received ideas, lecture notes, pointers to books and materials, the possibility to chat with other students on the course and thus exchange ideas, experiences and suggestions.

If you have a special interest, these are also catered for in the TESL-L list-serv. Once you have joined, you'll be able to take advantage of the smaller sub-groups which range from groups for teachers of young learners, through materials writers, a discussion of work conditions, CALL (Computer Assisted – or Aided – Language Learning), and many others.

Disadvantages of listservs

It's well-known that you can't please all of the people all the time – and a listserv is no exception. A lot of the discussions will have no relevance to your own work most of the time. I particularly remember a debate about techniques used to remember Korean surnames in large classes, which – of course – was very useful for some of the subscribers, but of absolutely no relevance to me. Some people see this as a disadvantage, but try to look on a listserv as a magazine: there are always some articles you just don't want to read.

If after a while you find that you are no longer interested in being subscribed to a certain group, you can find instructions on how to unsubscribe in the original welcome message you were sent when you first subscribed. Yet another good reason to hang on to it.

Using the Listserv

Once you have subscribed and received your confirmation, you will also begin to receive email messages from other list subscribers. Let's take a look at how this works ...

One member of the listserv in Japan (A) has suddenly been told she has to do a substitution class the following morning. It's an advanced level class (way above the level she is used to teaching) and she has no idea how to go about it. She sends an email message to the listserv asking for help. When the listserv receives the message, it automatically mails it to the 20,000 subscribers (B–E):

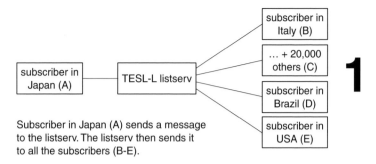

Subscriber in Japan (A) sends a message to the listserv. The listserv then sends it to all the subscribers (B-E).

Let's suppose a subscriber in Italy (B) has a great idea for the teacher in Japan. He can mail it directly to the teacher by using the email address in the teacher's original message:

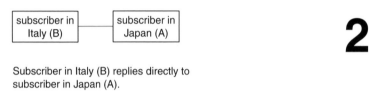

Subscriber in Italy (B) replies directly to subscriber in Japan (A).

A subscriber in Brazil (D) has an idea which she thinks everyone might like to know about, so she sends her reply to the listserv which then sends it on to all the subscribers again. And so it goes on:

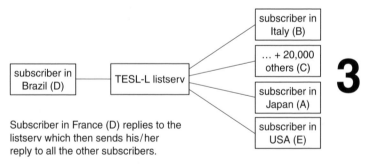

Subscriber in France (D) replies to the listserv which then sends his/her reply to all the other subscribers.

It's not unusual for new subscribers to just receive and read messages for a short while, until they get the 'feel' of the listserv – this is known as 'lurking', and is considered part of getting to know a new group of people.

TESL-L generates a limited number of messages each day. This is because it is a moderated list, meaning that messages posted to the list are vetted before they go further than the main computer. Having said this, it can still generate a fair bit of mail on a daily basis. The ***Listserv FAQ****s* section provides tips on how to control what you receive.

Student discussion lists

Student discussion lists are email mailing lists that have been set up specifically to allow students to contact each other and talk about subjects of mutual interest. These lists function in the same way as the teacher listservs above. Some example lists – all based at listserv@latrobe.edu.au – are:

BUSINESS-SL   Business and Economics
CHAT-SL   General conversation
DISCUSS-SL   Higher level conversation
EVENT-SL   Current Affairs
MOVIE-SL   Film and related themes
MUSIC-SL   Music and related themes
SCITECH-SL   Science and Technology
SPORT-SL   Sport and Games

These lists provide excellent opportunities for cross-cultural discussion between students. For more lists, see the *FAQs* section at the end of the book.

4.2 Listserv FAQs

DO I HAVE TO STAY CONNECTED ALL DAY TO RECEIVE THE MESSAGES?

Listserv messages are written at all times of the day by people all around the world. If you don't want to (or can't) stay connected all day, set your subscription to *digest* format (you'll find instructions in your original welcome message). This way, all the messages of the day are put together into one longer email message and simply mailed to you once a day.

WHAT IF I'M NOT INTERESTED IN ALL THE MESSAGES?

Set your subscription to *index* format. In this format, all you receive is a list of the subject lines of the messages of the day. If you are interested in receiving any of the messages, you then send off for them. Instructions are included in the welcome message.

I'M GOING AWAY ON HOLIDAY AND I DON'T WANT TO RETURN TO HUNDREDS OF EMAIL MESSAGES. CAN I STOP THEM WHILE I'M AWAY?

Set your subscription to *nomail* when you plan to be away for a while. This will stop listserv messages being sent to you and clogging up your mailbox. When you return, you can set it to *mail* again.

HANDS ON 📧

Why not subscribe to a couple of lists: one for professional purposes and one personal. (Use Liszt – http://www.liszt.com – to find lists which interest you.) Make sure you save the subscription confirmation and any rules and instructions you receive. Follow the discussions for a couple of days until you have a feel for the list, then send your first message. If after a while you find the list isn't helpful or useful to you, unsubscribe yourself.

4.3 Online chat

The term *chat* – when it is used in the field of the Internet – refers to synchronous (i.e. real time) communication between two or more people, using the keyboard as the means of communication. This can be contrasted with Internet *telephony*, which allows two people to speak to each other using the Internet, as with a normal telephone call.

At present, the infrastructure of most countries does not really allow for effective voice conversations over the Internet, nor does the speed of connection enjoyed by most people, so the only real way people can communicate in real time is to use the system known as Internet Relay Chat (IRC). These days IRC is a generic term for different ways of 'chatting', but in this section we're going to look at the original IRC.

My personal recommendation for an IRC program is mIRC (you can download it from TUCOWS at www.tucows.com). It's very compact, versatile and easy to manage.

When you first start up mIRC, you will need to enter some personal information and choose a 'nickname' by which you wish to be known.

You should bear in mind that there are a lot of people out there on the Net using IRC. Your chosen nickname might already be taken. When you try to connect, mIRC will tell you if your nickname is taken, and will give you 60 seconds to change it before 'killing you' (not as painful as it sounds!). To change your nickname, type: /nick *new_nickname*

Join a channel

A channel is a 'place' on IRC where group conversations occur. People can join the same channel and see each other. Depending on its topic and time of the day a channel can be very crowded. On the large IRC Networks (DALnet) as many as 2,000 channels can exist. Whenever you want to refer to a channel's name, it should be prefixed with a '#' or '&'. You also need to use the name, including the '#', to join a channel, to leave it, to set its parameters, etc.

Some of the (over 2,000) channels available on DALnet

When you have all this information, the first thing you can do (if you don't know who you want to talk to) is get the channel list. Just click the *List channels* icon on the toolbar, and watch as a huge list of channels starts appearing. Be warned – there are some very offensive channels out there!

Choose a channel you want to join, and type the following in the text entry window at the bottom of the program /join *#channel_name* . A new window will open with a list of names of those people currently talking in your chosen channel. Once you get to the channel, you will see people talking. It will probably look like this:

{ Gavin }	Anybody seen the Puzzlemaker site?
{ Gavin }	http://www.puzzlemaker.com ?
{ Emily }	No. What is it?
{ Gavin }	Makes online wordsearches, crosswords, etc
{ Dick }	Good ... slow, though!
{ Emily }	Really?
{ Gavin }	Can be, but worth the wait
{ Emily }	Level?
{ Gavin }	All, really. V. easy to use

Note that you will often come in during the middle of a conversation. Unless you're familiar with the channel you may want to sit and watch it for a minute or two to see what the conversation is about. Often the channel name (for instance, #Twilight_Zone) has nothing to do with what conversation goes on on the channel (#Twilight_Zone doesn't have discussions about the TV show "Twilight Zone").

To start talking, just type! And when you're done saying what you have to say, just hit the *Return* key. You can start with something simple like 'hello!'. You don't have to type *<nickname> hello!* because IRC will insert *<nickname>* before all of your messages.

In the channel window that opens once you join a channel you'll see an alphabetical list of people that are on the channel on the right side of the window.

Basic commands

The forward slash (/) is the default command character. Commands on IRC are not case sensitive, and can be abbreviated to their first letters. Anything that does not begin with "/" is assumed to be a message to someone and will be sent to your current channel, or to a person you are chatting with in a private chat.

Here is a list of basic commands:

/help	shows general help or help on the given command
/list	lists all current channels
/join	to join a channel

/part	to leave a channel (same as LEAVE)
/quit	exits your IRC session (same as BYE and EXIT)
/nick	changes your nickname
/away	leaves a message saying you're away or not paying attention
/whois	displays information about someone
/invite	sends an invitation to another user
/kick	gets rid of someone on a channel
/me	sends anything about you to a channel or QUERY

Once in a channel, if you find someone you think you'd like to have a chat with, but would like to do it away from the hustle and bustle of the main channel, click on their name in the user window on the right, then right click and choose *Query*. This opens up a private channel between you and the person you have queried. Note that you are still technically talking in the original channel. Since it is equally possible for people to query you, you should keep your eye on the button bars at the bottom to see if any other private channels open up while you are talking on a channel.

The world of IRC is chaotic and anarchic, and you will probably not find many channels of use. However, given the fact that you can create your own private chat rooms, it is an ideal place to arrange for groups of students to meet up and talk to each other.

There are many other chat programs on the market. Below are a couple that I have found useful both for teaching and personal use:

ICQ (I Seek You!) www.mirabilis.com

This free program allows users to send text messages and files to each other (this is known as Instant Messaging, and is similar to email) as well as to chat in real time. It is very popular, with millions of users, and has the advantage of being very easy to use and much more controllable than IRC. If you want to try it out, download it from the address above and install it, then search for me – my ICQ number is 32052080.

Microsoft Comic Chat (www.microsoft.com)

This is also free, and a big hit with young learners and teenagers. The program comes as standard with Internet Explorer. Students type their conversations in a simple text box, then the program represents the conversation as a comic strip as it builds.

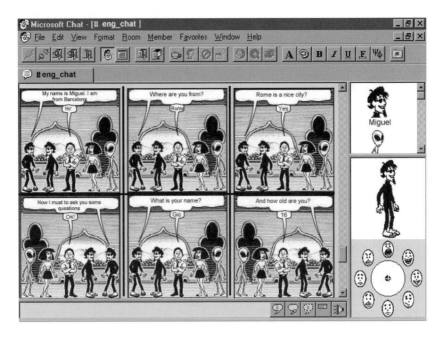

Programs such as Comic Chat can, of course, be used in place of the more traditional email approach in a student penpal exchange. Live chat is always more satisfying than sending and waiting for messages by email. However, if you choose this option, you should be aware that there are far more things that can go wrong, from not being able to get a connection to the Internet (and that could happen at either end of the operation) to not being able to control the language produced on all the computers. Where I work, we have found it to be a useful addition to a penpal exchange, allowing students to really appreciate that there is 'someone at the other end of the line'.

4.4 Browser caching

In **Section 1** we looked at the idea of visiting websites with your web browser just before you use them in class. This saves a copy of the pages and images on your computer and makes it much quicker to return to them in class time.

If you find that you are doing this, but you are still having to wait a long time for pages to display, it's possible that your browser cache is not large enough. If you want to increase the quantity of space set aside on your computer for webpages, try the following:

In *Netscape* go to *Edit*, select *Preferences* then *Advanced* and then choose *Cache*. From there you can increase or decrease the memory and disk caches or empty them totally. It's impossible to say what the correct amount is, but it's sensible to double the numbers in the two boxes and then see if it makes a difference. This means increasing the memory cache to 2048 Kbs (Kilobytes) and the disk cache to 10,000. You can increase these numbers a lot more than this until you are happy with the performance you are getting.

In *Explorer* go to *View* and then choose *Internet Options*. On the first screen, click the *Settings* button in the *Temporary Internet Files*. From there you can increase or decrease the amount of disk space to use in Mb (Megabytes). Again, only a fair amount of web browsing will tell you how much disk space you need. I usually have mine set to about 50Mb, which is a lot of web information.

Obviously there are plenty of other things to do on the Internet, but it is beyond the scope of this book to go into any real detail. Those of you who are interested in further investigation might like to start by looking into the area of newsgroups (download Free Agent – available from TUCOWS at http://www.tucows.com – or Outlook Express).

5 FAQs

In this FAQs section you will find reference material and sample sheets for some of the activities recommended in this book.

5.0 Connecting to the Internet

How do I get connected to the Internet?

To connect your computer to the Internet you will need:

- a modem in your computer linked to your phone line
- an Internet Service Provider (ISP)

A modem is a piece of equipment which allows your computer to communicate with other computers across a telephone connection. There are two types of modem – internal and external. There is little difference between the two types, although external ones are usually easier to install and configure. Make sure you get a fast modem to ensure fast access to the Internet. Any good computer shop should be able to recommend a selection.

An ISP is a company which has powerful computers permanently connected to the Internet. When you use your computer to dial your ISP, they allow you to use their connection to the Internet to send and receive information. Don't forget that in most countries you will be paying phone charges while you are connected to your ISP, so make sure you subscribe to a local company.

It is relatively easy to connect to the Internet. When you have subscribed to an ISP and have all your account details, install Microsoft Internet Explorer or Netscape Communicator from a CD (you can often get these from computer magazines) and follow the instructions. Explorer should automatically configure your machine to connect to the Internet and all you have to do is answer the questions asked by the installation software, using the information given by your ISP. If this doesn't work, take a look at the information on this page (you'll need to use a friend's connection!): http://www.internet-connections.net/ic/users/manuals/win95.setup.dial-up-net.html

5.1 Internet terminology

I find the terminology and acronyms on the Internet difficult – it looks like I have to learn a whole new language. What do they all mean?

There's a lot of jargon involved in using the Internet. This short list covers the main terms which come up in this book and introduces some other common ones which you're likely to encounter when on the Net.

Application   A piece of software that performs a useful function.

Archive   A file (or files) that have been compressed to form one smaller file. Software distributed on the Net is usually archived.

Attachment   A file sent together with an email message. See *Section 1*.

Bookmark   A way of saving a web address for future reference (also called Favorites). See *Section 1*.

Bounce   When email is returned due to a delivery failure. See *Section 1*.

Browser   A program like Internet Explorer or Netscape Navigator which displays webpages. See *Section 1*.

Cache   Recently visited webpages stored on your computer. See *Section 1*.

CALL   Computer Assisted (or Aided) Language Learning. (See also TELL.)

Chat   The part of the Internet used to communicate in real time by typing messages to one or more other people. See *Section 4*.

Cross post   To send the same message to more than one list or newsgroup.

Dial-up   To connect to the Net using a computer modem and phone line.

Download   The transfer of a file from one computer to another over the Net.

Email   Electronic Mail. A method of sending messages via computer. See *Section 1*.

Emoticons (also Smileys)   A facial expression made using punctuation, e.g. :-) These are used in email and chat to communicate feelings or emotions. They must be viewed sideways on to get the full effect.

Encryption   A method of coding information to prevent unauthorised access. Most common in online shopping for sending credit card details.

FAQs   Frequently Asked Questions. You will find FAQs all over the Net. Their purpose is to provide easy access to the most common questions related to an issue.

FTP   File Transfer Protocol. A method of transferring files from one computer to another.

Hardware   The physical components of a computer: screen, monitor, etc.

Homepage   The main page of a website. See *Section 1*.

Host   A computer which holds information on the Internet. Most commonly seen in browser error message: *Host Not Found*.

HTML   Hypertext Mark-Up Language. The language used to write a web document. See *Section 3*.

ICQ   A popular Internet chat and message program. See *Section 4*.

IRC   Internet Relay Chat allows a group of people to chat in real time over the Net. See *Section 4*.

ISP   Internet Service Provider. The company which helps you to connect to the Internet. See *Sections 1* and *4*.

Link   A piece of text or image on a webpage which, when clicked on, takes the user to another page or website. See *Section 1*.

LISTSERV   An automated mailing list distribution system. See *Section 4*.

Lurking   Subscribing to a listserv or newsgroup but not participating.

Mailing list   An automated email system similar to a listserv.

Modem   A piece of hardware which allows two or more computers to communicate with each other using normal phone lines. See *Section 1*.

Netiquette   The etiquette of Internet usage. See *Section 1*.

Newbie   A newcomer to the Internet – used as a term of ridicule.

Newsgroup   A message area defined by subject matter. There are over 30,000 newsgroups. Similar to listservs and mailing lists, they are usually more 'anarchic' in content. Software called a newsreader is needed to subscribe to and read newsgroups.

Shareware   Software which is generally available in a 'try-before-you-buy' form.

Software   Programs installed and run on a computer.

Spam   An unsolicited email message sent to lots of people.

TELL   Technology Enhanced Language Learning. This covers all aspects of using technology in language instruction, as opposed to the more limited field of CALL which refers exclusively to the use of computers.

Video-conferencing   A form of audio-visual communication on the Internet. You need a video camera, sound card and a fast Internet connection.

Webpage   One screen of information on the Internet. See *Section 1*.

Website   A collection of webpages built around a common theme. See *Section 1*.

World Wide Web   A hypertext information and resource system for the Internet. See *Section 1*.

5.2 Selected websites

Where can I publish my students' work?

These sites all offer free web space:

http://www.geocities.com
http://www.tripod.com
http://www.angelfire.com
http://www.xoom.com

Where can I get email addresses for my students?

These sites offer free web-based email. They can be very slow and unreliable depending on the time of day and where in the world you are accessing them from. Their real disadvantage, however, is that they require you to be connected a lot of the time while you are reading and writing email. Clever users will save messages to disk before disconnecting and reading them offline, as well as writing new messages before connecting and pasting them into the webmail message window.

http://mail.yahoo.com
http://www.hotmail.com
http://www.netaddress.com
http://www.egroups.com

Where can I get information about making webpages?

http://www.tucows.com
http://www.netscape.com
http://www.download.com
http://www.clipartdownload.com
http://www.webmonkey.com
http://www.aplusart.simplenet.com/aplusart/
http://www.ist.net/clipart
http://www.aitech.ac.jp/~iteslj/Articles/Kelly-MakePage/
http://www.xlrn.ucsb.edu/~hshetzer/web/
http://www.davesite.com/Webstation/html/
http://Web.uvic.ca/hrd/halfbaked/

Where can I find useful sites for teaching?

Here is a selection of sites I have found useful for dealing with various topicc areas:

CALL

http://www.athel.com . . . . Athelstan Online
http://www.latrobe.edu.au/www/education/celia/celia.html . CELIA Computer Enhanced
Language Instruction Archive
http://www.cti.hull.ac.uk/eurocall/ecabout.htm. . . . . Euro CALL
http://citt.marin.cc.ca.us/using.html . . . . Center for Internet Technology
in Teaching
http://www.december.com/cmc/mag/index.html . . . . Computer-Mediated
Communication Magazine
http://llt.msu.edu/ . . . . Language learning and
technology

Company/Business/ESP Pages

http://www.lydbury.co.uk/besig . . . . The IATEFL Business English SIG
http://www.languagekey.com. . . . . The Language Key Magazine
http://www.bized.ac.uk . . . . Biz/ed resources for students, teachers
and lecturers
http://www.eleaston.com/biz/bizhome.html . . . . Business English online
http://www.eslcafe.com/search/Business_English/ . . . Dave's ESL Café business section

EFL/ESL/FLT

http://www.net-language.com . . . . The ezine for teachers and students of English
http://its-online.com . . . . Another printed and web-based EFL magazine
http://www.englishnow.co.uk. . . . . English Now!
http://www.eslcafe.com . . . . Dave Sperling's ESL Cafe
http://www.baysights.com/aardvark/ . . . . Aadvark's EFL resources
http://www.stuff.co.uk/wicked.htm. . . . . Wicked Stuff for English Learners
http://www.englishtown.com. . . . . EF EnglishTown
http://www.yahoo.com/Education/Languages/English_as_a_Second_Language. . . . .
Yahoo section
http://www.linguistic-funland.com . . . . Kristina Pfaff's Linguistic Funland
http://members.tripod.com/~towerofenglish . . The Tower of English
http://www.esl-lab.com . . . . Randall's ESL Cyber Listening Lab
http://www.englishlistening.com . . . . The English Listening Lounge Language
Resources on the Web

History

http://www.thehistorychannel.co.uk/index.htm. . . . . . The History Channel UK
http://digischool.bart.nl/en/royA.html. . . . . royA History Links
http://history.evansville.net/referenc.html . . . . History references and resources
http://www.ed.gov/pubs/parents/History/Story.html . . Activities, history as story

Jobs

http://www.jobs.edunet.com/iatefl/ . . IATEFL Electronic Jobshop
http://www.tefl.com/jobs/ . . . . TEFL Professional Network
http://eslcafe.com/jobs. . . . . Dave's ESL Cafe jobs page

Language - Reference

http://www.travlang.com/languages . . . . Foreign languages for travellers
http://www.facstaff.bucknell.edu/rbeard/diction.html . . . . . . A Web of online dictionaries
http://titania.cobuild.collins.co.uk . . . . COBUILD Dictionary homepage
http://humanities.uchicago.edu/forms_unrest/ROGET.html . . Roget's Thesaurus
http://62.6.162.42/intro.html . . . . An Elementary Grammar
http://www.edunet.com/english/grammar/index.html. . . . . . Online English Grammar
http://www.m-w.com/netdict.htm . . . . Webster Dictionary
http://deil.lang.uiuc.edu . . . . University of Illinois
LinguaCenter

Miscellaneous

http://www.encarta.msn.com/encartahome.asp . . Microsoft Encarta Encyclopaedia
. . . . homepage
http://www.auschron.com/mrpants . . . . Mr Smarty Pants knows...
http://www.guinnessrecords.com. . . . . Guinness World Records
http://www.britannica.com . . . . The Encyclopaedia Britannica
http://www.bbc.co.uk. . . . . The official BBC homepage

Movies

http://www.script-o-rama.com. . Drew's Script-o-Rama
http://www.hollywood.com . . . . Hollywood Site
http://www.imdb.com . . . . The Internet movie database
http://www.disney.com . . . . Disney homepage
http://www.cinema1.com . . . . . The e-Zine for movies
http://www.film.com . . . . Movie reviews, news, trailers...

Museums

http://www.louvre.fr . . . . The Louvre, Paris
http://www.nga.gov . . . . National Gallery of Art
http://wwar.com . . . . Worldwide arts resources
http://www.arca.net/uffizi . . . . . The Uffizi Gallery in Florence
http://www.nmsi.ac.uk/ . . . . National Museum of Science and Industry
http://www.si.edu/start.htm. . . . Smithsonian Institution
http://www.paris.org/Musees/ . . The Museums of Paris
http://www.nhm.ac.uk/ . . . . . . The Natural History Museum

Music

http://www.lyrics.ch/index.htm . . . . The international lyrics server
http://www.mtv.com . . . . MTV
http://www.rockhall.com . . . . The Rock Hall, Cleveland
http://lenny.dyadel.net/lyrics.htm . . . . Always on the run lyrics page
http://www.yahoo.com/Entertainment/Music/Groups. . The Groups page at Yahoo
http://www.qonline.co.uk . . . . Q Magazine Online
http://www.nme.com/ . . . . The New Musical Express
http://www.ubl.com/ . . . . Music's homepage

News

http:www.yahoo.com/headlines. . Yahoo News
http://www.crayon.net. . . . . Create your free newspaper
http://www.cbs.com . . . . CBS News
http://www.4-d.co.uk . . . . The Times
http://www.newsdirectory.com . . English language media online
http://www.newspapers.com . . . Newspapers online
http://www.bbc.co.uk . . . . The official BBC homepage
http://www.cnn.com . . . . CNN

Organisations

http://www.britcoun.org . . The British Council
http://www.iatefl.org. . . . . IATEFL
http://www.tesol.edu . . . . TESOL
http://www.calico.org . . . . Computer Assisted Language Instruction Consortium
http://www.cal.org . . . . . . Center for Applied Linguistics

Penpals

http://www.iecc.org/related-resources.html . . . . Classroom connection resources
http://www.penpals.com. . . . . PenPals
http://its-online.com/meetnow.html. its-online EFL magazine penpals page
http://www.britcoun.org.hk/epals/epals_new.html. . . . . Epals
http://ilc2.doshisha.ac.jp/users/kkitao/online/www/keypal.htm. . Keypal opportunities for students

Politics / Government

http://www.parliament.uk . . . The British Parliament
http://www.royal.gov.uk . . . . . The British Monarchy
http://www.open.gov.uk. . . . . UK public sector information
http://www.whitehouse.gov . . The Whitehouse
http://www.foe.co.uk/. . . . . . . Friends of the Earth
http://www.greenpeace.org . . Greenpeace

Search pages

http://www.yahoo.com . . . . Yahoo
http://www.altavista.com . . AltaVista
http://www.excite.com . . . . Excite
http://www.lycos.com . . . . . Lycos
http://www.askjeeves.com. . Ask Jeeves

Sport

http://www.nba.com . . . . The National Basketball Association
http://www.sydney.olympic.org. . . . . The Sydney 2000 Olympics website
http://www.ioc.org. . . . . The International Olympic Committee
http://www.sportsnetwork.com/ . . . . The Sports Network
http://www.tns.lcs.mit.edu/cgi-bin/sports . . World Wide Web of Sports

Student writing

http://www.ihes.com/Sresource/ . . . . Student written online magazine at IH Barcelona
http://deil.lang.uiuc.edu/exchange/ . . . . ExChange ESL Magazine
http://darkwing.uoregon.edu/~leslieob/pizzaz.html . . . . . . Pizzaz writing project
http://www.otan.dni.us/webfarm/emailproject/email.htm. . Email projects homepage

Travel and tourism

http://www.travlang.com/languages . . . Foreign languages for travellers
http://travelsearch.com. . . . . Travel industry search engine
http://www15.pair.com/cir/index.html. . The UK travel guide
http://www.dedas.com/hm-usa . . . . HM USA travel guide

Younger learners

http://www.bonus.com . . . . Bonus.Com - games for kids
http://www.ajkids.com . . . . Ask Jeeves search engine for
kids
http://www.yahooligans.com . . . . Yahoo Search engine for kids
http://www.lycoszone.com . . . . Lycos Search engine for Kids
http://www.youngcommonwealth.org . . . . Young Commonwealth
http://www.thepotters.com/puzzles.html . . . . John's wordsearch puzzles
http://www.pathfinder.com/TFK/ - . . . . TIME for kids
http://zeus.informatik.uni-frankfurt.de/%7Efp/Disney/Lyrics/ . Disney song lyrics

5.3 Starting a website review file

What do I do when I find a good website?

Firstly, don't forget to *Bookmark* the site or add it to your *Favorites*. Then, write a short review of the site for your colleagues or students – this will help them find what they are looking for. I maintain a file of website reviews which are classified by topic and level – this makes it easier for other teachers to find useful material, and for me to keep track of the sites I like to use. A good review can be far more useful than an obscure entry in your *Favorites* or *Bookmarks*.

Here is a sample site review form. This does not claim to be the definitive form, but it should serve as a basis for your own reviews.

Website review form

GENERAL INFO	
Name of site	
URL of site	
Date visited	
Reviewer	
SITE SUMMARY	
Description Add a short description of the site	
Content summary Give a brief summary of the contents of the site	
SITE DETAILS	
Information Is the site content correct, reliable and accurate? Is the writer an expert in this subject?	
Currency Is the site up-to-date? When was new information last added? When were the pages last updated?	
Content Is the content interesting, relevant, funny, useful or entertaining? How would you describe it?	
Presentation Is it attractive and easy to navigate? Does it use a lot of graphics, sound or multimedia files?	
Functionality Does it all work? Are there any broken links or missing pages? Does it take a long time to display pages?	
VERDICT	
	Excellent ( ) Very good ( ) Good ( ) Average ( ) Poor ( )

5.4 **Publishing student material**

How do I protect myself and my students from possible unwelcome consequences of publishing course work on the Internet?

Apart from not publishing material owned by other people, there has been a lot of discussion in academic circles about the use of student work on websites. Most teachers have tended to suppose that they can simply put student writing on their own (or school) website without any problems. After a lengthy discussion on many of the academic listservs it is now considered wise (and ethical) to secure permission from students to publish before actually putting content onto the web.

Here is a sample release form for students to sign, giving the school or institution permission to use their work on the website. This constitutes a basic agreement between the student and the school in which the student agrees to allow written material produced by them to be published on the website without the problem of copyright cropping up. It's a good idea to find out if any students are likely to have a problem with their work being published on the Internet before starting work on a project. Any form of this nature cannot take into account local conditions and regulations, so this should be taken as a simple suggestion only.

Student release form

STUDENT INFORMATION	
Name:	....
Address:	....
	....
	....
Tel. no:	....

PROJECT INFORMATION	
School or institution:	....
Project description:	....
Release details:	....
	....
	....
	....
	NOTE: Specify if the student work can be used for general publishing, school or institution publicity, etc.

AUTHORISATION	
For the student:	Signature: ....
	Name: ....
	Note: If the student is under 18, this form must be signed by a parent or legal guardian.
On behalf of the school:	Signature: ....
	Name: ....
Date:	....

Recommended resources

Corio, R. and Meloni, C. (1995) 'The guidelines net project', *CAELL Journal* 6/3.

Darby, J. and Joyce, M. (July 1995) 'Using the Internet for Teaching', *Active Learning 2.*

Eastment, D. (April 1996) 'The Internet for Teachers and Learners', *Modern English Teacher*, 5, 2.

Gibbs, M. and Smith, R. (1993) *Navigating the Internet*, Sams Publishing.

Howard, R. and McGrath, I. (eds.) (1995) *Distance Education for Language Teachers*, Multilingual Matters Ltd.

Krol, E. (1994) *The Whole Internet User's Guide and Catalog*, Ca: O'Reilly and Associates.

Lake, D.T. (1995) 'What is the Internet? – Answering the Teacher's Question', *Learning and Leading with Technology*

Levine, J. (1996) *Internet for Dummies*, International Data Group Books.

Marine, A., Kirkpatrick, S., Neou, V. and Warc, C. (1993) *Internet: Getting Started*, Prentice-Hall.

Motteram, G. (February 1996) 'The Internet for ELT: A newbie's guide', *IATEFL Newsletter.*

NCET (ed.) (1995) *Highways for Learning: An Introduction to the Internet*, Coventry: NCET.

Pickering, J. (1995) 'Teaching on the Internet is Learning', *Active Learning 2.*

Rice, C.D. (January 1996) 'Bring intercultural encounters into classrooms', *THE Journal*, **60**.

Sperling, D. (1997) *The Internet Guide for English Language Teachers*, Prentice-Hall.

Warschauer, M. (1995) *E-mail for English teaching*, TESOL.

Index

abbreviations, in email 13, 14
access
    control of 34
    free to the Internet 5
    speed of 3, 32
    temporarily unobtainable 9
    to computers 31–2
Acrobat Reader 148, 150
activities 37–127
    by level 37–8
    by theme 38
addresses
    accuracy in typing 6, 9, 13
    in email 12, 13
adjectives 69–71, 74–5, 77–9, 126–7
    comparatives 118–20
    superlatives 118–20
Adobe Acrobat 150
advanced learners, activities for 38
advanced Net 148–61
advice, giving 43–4, 44–6, 81–2, 120–1
agreeing 59–60, 109–10
alphabet 106–7
AltaVista 17–18, 20, 22
    compared with *Yahoo!* 24–5
    free web graphics 139
    machine translation service 22
American English, and British English 64–5
Angelfire 141
animals 108–9
anti-virus packages *see* virus protection
    software
Arachnophilia webpage design program 135
archive facility 152
arrangements, making 84–5, 88–90
art 97–8
Ask Jeeves 25–6
Ask Jeeves Kids 27
asterisk, in searches 22
astrology 74–5
attachments
    email 15
    unsolicited 16
    virus warning in email 16
audio 32, 148, 149

backing up material 33
BBC site 27
bilingual exchange, guidelines 130–1
bilingual websites 143
biographies 49–50, 68–9, 97–8
bold text, in webpages 135, 136, 139
Bookmarks 8, 18
books, reading 66–7
Boolean Operators 20–1
borrowings, in English 62–4
bouncing 13
British English, and American English 64–5
browser caching 160
browsers
    choosing 4, 9
    email direct from 10
    enhancements 148–50
    free of charge 5
    how to download 5
    to view your own webpage 136
business classes 30
Business English, activities for 37, 38
business publications 30
business students, webpage projects for 143
BUSINESS-SL 155

caching 32–3, 160–1
CALL (Computer Assisted – or Aided –
    Language Learning) 152, 153
capital letters
    and Netiquette 16
    in webpage file names 141
celebrations 100–1
censorship 35
channels
    joining for chat 156–8
    list of 157
chat, online 156–60
chat programs 159–60
CHAT-SL 155
cinema 57–9, 88–90, 146
class project, webpage 144–5
classroom
    access to computers 31–2
    computer room layouts 31–2

classroom (*cont.*)
  keeping control with the Internet 34
  layouts on *TESL-L* 31
  management techniques on *TSEL-L* 31
  questionable content on the Internet 34–6
  using the Internet in the 29–36
clothing 93–5
collaborative projects 30, 143
  deadlines in 147
colours 108–9, 113–15
  changing your webpage 140
Comic Chat 159
computer room layouts 31–2
computers
  activities 39–41, 41–2, 81–2, 117–18, 126–7
  ratio per student 31
  tools for connecting to the Internet 3–4
  use in the classroom 29–32
computing skills, basic 30, 147
conditionals 115–16
content, policing questionable 34–6
control, access 34
conversational skills 54–5
copyright 2, 134, 147
Copyright Website 147
corporate websites 30
countries 85–7, 113–15
country codes 6, 28
cultural differences 131
cursor, change to pointing finger 7
custom software 34
CyberPatrol 35
CyberSitter 35

DALnet 157
Dave's ESL Café
  EFL resources 29
  Student Email Connection 130
decisions, supporting 51–2
dedicated email programs 10
describing people or things 49–50, 74–5, 76–7, 77–9, 91–2, 93–5
Director Shockwave see Shockwave
disagreeing 59–60, 84–5, 109–10
DISCUSS-SL 155
discussion lists 8
  student 155
discussion pages 29
downloading
  free browsers 5
  in preparation for a class 32, 33
Dreamweaver 135

e-mail *see* email
educational listservs 151–5
EFL resources 28–9

EFL sites, penpal pages 128
Electronic Telegraph 6, 28
Electronic Freedom Foundation 147
electronic mail *see* email
electronic penpals 129
elementary learners, activities for 37
email 3, 10–15
  abbreviations in 13, 14
  attachments 15, 16
  causing offence by 16
  checking for new mail 11, 13
  connecting to the Net 11
  conventions of writing 12–13, 14
  dedicated programs 10
  deleting messages 10–11, 13
  disconnecting from the Net 11
  FAQs 16–17
  filing in another folder 13–14
  from your browser 10
  junk mail 16
  mailboxes 10–11
  opening attached files 15
  penpal exchanges *see* penpal exchanges
  personalising 10–11, 14
  policing for questionable content 36
  printing out messages 13
  reading new mail 11, 13
  replying to mail 11, 13
  sending files 15
  sending homework to teacher by 30
  sending messages 11, 12
  student discussion lists 155
  teaching by 153
  virus warning 16
  working *offline* 11, 13
  writing new messages 11–13
email mailing lists *see* listservs
English
  expressions used in everyday 62–4
  teaching material in 1
entertainment 109–10
error messages 9
Eudora 10
  Nicknames 12
  signature 14
Eudora Light 10
EVENT-SL 155
exchange, bilingual 130
Excite 27
explanations, giving 110–12
Explorer (Microsoft Internet) 4, 9, 148
  browser caching 160
  Favorites 8, 18
  free plug-ins 148
  Frontpage Express 136

open your own new webpage 137
Temporary Internet Files 36, 161

facts and figures 53–4, 108–9
FAQs
   email 16–17
   Listserv 155
   searching the Internet 28
   website 8–9
Favorites 8, 18
festivals 143
films *see* cinema
Flash 148
food and drink 79–80, 142
foreign language resources, links 29
foreign languages, searches in 20
foreign words 62–4
formatting text 135
frames 9
Free Agent 161
Frequently Asked Questions *see* FAQs

games 98–9, 118–20
Geocities 141
GIFs 35, 138–9
graphics 138–9
guidelines 3–36

help pages 19, 20, 27
holidays 61–2, 69–71, 71–3, 84–5, 87–8, 95–6,
   100–1
home/house 92–3, 115–16
homepages 7
   personal 33
homework, sending by email 30
HTML (Hypertext Mark-Up Language) 134,
   136–8
HTML tags 135
   closing tag 135
   opening tag 135
   and what they do 138
humour 146
hyperlink 7
hypertext links 7, 18
   adding to webpages 140–1
Hypertext Mark-Up Language *see* HTML

ICQ (I Seek You!) 159
images
   adding to webpages 138–9
   finding 28
IMG tag 138–9
imperatives 81–2, 120–1
in-company classes 30
informal language, use in emails 12–13, 14
Infoseek 27

Instant Messaging 159–60
instructions, giving 120–1
intermediate learners
   activities for lower- 37
   activities for mid- 37
   activities for upper- 37
International House Barcelona, on the Web 6–8
Internet 1
   activities 39–41, 41–3, 81–2, 117–18, 126–7
   addresses 6, 9, 13
   advanced 148–61
   as classroom tool 29–36
   free access to the 5
   preparation for class 30–3
   as resource bank 28–9
   searching *see* searching the Internet
   supervision of use 34–6
   terminology 10, 163
Internet Explorer, Microsoft *see* Explorer
Internet magazines 5
Internet Relay Chat (IRC) 156
Internet service provider (ISP) 4
inventions 125–6
inverted commas, in searches 22
IRC (Internet Relay Chat) 156–7
   basic commands 158–9
   nicknames 157
ISDN adapter card 3
ISDN phone line 3
ISP *see* Internet service provider (ISP)
issues, local or national 144
italicised text, in web pages 139
its-online 29, 128

JPGs 35, 138–9
junk mail 16

keyboard, use to move up and down webpage 8
language 62–4, 64–5
language learning resources, links 29
language teachers 1, 150–5
languages other than English, searches in 20
lesson
   ideas 29
   preparation for Internet 30–3
likes and dislikes 79–80, 88–90
links, 5, 7
   finding 28
   inserting in webpages 140–1
   slowness of 9
   to search engines 146
   updated lists of useful 29
listservs 15, 28, 130, 151–6
   advantages of 152–3
   controlling what you receive 155–6
   database of 152

listservs (*cont.*)
  digest format for 155
  disadvantages of 153
  educational 143
  index format for 155
  joining 151
  stopping while on holiday with *nomail* 155
  for students 155
  subgroups 153
  for teachers 150–5
  unsubscribing 152
  using 153–4
Liszt, list of listservs 152
logos 73–4
lurking 154
Lycos 27

McAfee 16
machine translation service, in *AltaVista* 22
Macintosh computers 4
Macromedia
  Dreamweaver 135
  Shockwave Flash Player 148
mailing lists 143, 146, 150–5
  see also listservs
Microsoft
  Comic Chat 160
  Frontpage Express 135
  Internet Explorer *see* Explorer
  Word 9, 15, 134
Microsoft site 27
mIRC 156
modem 3
mouse, using the 30
MOVIE-SL 155
multimedia 32
  and plug-ins 148–50
music 46–7, 68–9
MUSIC-SL 155
mystery 106–7, 110–12

names 113–15, 123–4
nationalities 85–7, 113–15
Net *see* Internet
Net Language 29
Net Nanny 35
NETEACH-L 130, 152
Netiquette 14, 16
NetPals 130
Netscape (Communicator) 4, 9, 137, 148
  Bookmarks 8, 18
  browser caching 161
  Cache 36
  editor 134
  free plug-ins 148
  Page Composer 136, 142

news 54–5, 55–7, 105–6, 143
newsgroups 161
newspapers, published on the Net 150
nicknames, in Internet Relay Chat (IRC) 156
Norton AntiVirus 16
Notepad 135, 136, 138
numbers 53–4, 106–7

occupations 77–9
offensive words, database to check for 35
offline, working with email 11, 13
online chat 156–60
  basic commands 158–9
  joining a channel 157–8
Open Text 27
operators
  Boolean 20–1
  Proximity 21
  in searches 20–1
opinions, giving 59–60, 97–8
ordering and prioritising 51–2
Outlook Express 10
  newsgroups 161

page caching 32–3
parents, release form for student publication on
    the Net 134, 135
passives 125–6
password-protection 34
passwords
  setting 35
  start-up 34
PDF files 150
penpal exchanges 31, 128–33
  and *Comic Chat* 159
  examples 131–2
  finding partners 130
  guidelines 130–1
  starting off 128–9
  tips 132–3
penpal pages, at EFL sites 128
people, famous 48–9, 49–50, 51–2, 68–9, 97–8,
    112–13, 123–4, 125–6, 146
personal homepages 33
personal information, publishing of student on
    the Net 134, 135
personality 74–5, 76–7
plug-ins 148–50
policing content 34–6
  practical approach 35–6
  software approach 35
predictions, making 73–5, 110–12
preparation for Internet class 30–3
printing out
  email messages 13
  part of a website 9

a Web page 8, 9
problems
with changing material in sites 33
of finding material 1, 27, 28
junk mail 16
with technology breaks 33
temporarily unobtainable access 9
virus warning 16
processes, describing 79–80
programs, for making webpages 135–6
projects 128–47
Web-based 134–47
Proximity Operators 21
publishing 133–4
ethics in 134
websites 141–2
punctuation, in searches 22
puzzles 98–9, 118–20

questionable content, policing 34–6
questions
direct and indirect 44–6
forms 41–3, 118–20
to ask before searching the Web 19
to the browser 26
quizzes 98–9, 118–20
quotations 112–13

Real Audio 148, 149
real language search pages 19, 25–7
Real Player see Real Audio
reasoning 110–12
reasons, giving 51–2
release form for student publication on the Net
134, 135, 173
reported speech 43–4
research, doing and reporting on 117–18
resource bank, Internet as a 28–9
reviewing, websites, 126–7, 170–1
rhymes 117–18
Rich Text Format *see* RTF files
RTF files, for sending email attachments 15

saving
documents as HTML 134
multimedia files 32
SCITECH-SL 155
scroll bar 8
search engines 17–18, 19, 19–22
alternatives to 27
comparison of 24–7
inadequacies of 27, 28
submitting a link to 146
search sites, help pages 19, 20, 27
searches
in languages other than English 20

nesting 20
operators in 20–1
problems 1, 27, 28
punctuation in 22
refining 19–22
symbols used (+ and −) 20, 28
searching the Internet 17–27
FAQs 28
making search choices 27
refining searches using a search engine 18,
19–22
search types 19–27
strategies for subject guides 23–5
using 'real language' search sites 25–7
service provider *see* Internet service provider
(ISP)
services for publishing websites, free 141
shapes 113–15
Shockwave 148, 149
shopping 91–2
software
non-vital 34
which policies questionable content 35
which requires user identification 34
sound files 32, 148, 149
space, increasing for webpages 161
specialist subjects, listservs 151
speed
of access 3, 32
of connections 9
slowness of links 9
sport 82–3
SPORT-SL 155
storing *see* caching
story telling 54–5, 144
student discussion lists 155
student work, publishing on the Net 133–4
students
contact with other 30
listservs for 155
subject guides 19, 23–5
Yahoo! 23–5
suggesting 84–5, 109–10
supervision, of Internet use 34–6
SurfWatch 35
survival 120–1
synonyms 117–18

teachers
email contact 28
list of useful sites 165–70
listservs for 150–4
mailing lists 150–5
own sites 29
teaching, by email 153
teaching material, finding 1, 28

technology breaks 33
teenagers 43–4, 122–3
telephone line 3
telephony, Internet 156
television 59–60, 144
templates 135
   models for webpages 135, 142, 145
tenses
   conditionals 115–16
   future 61–2
   mixed past 82–3
   past 48–50, 51–2, 61–2, 69–71, 71–3, 125–6
   present continuous 76–7
   present perfect 49–50, 69–71
terminology, Internet 10, 161
TESL-L (Teachers of English as a Second
    Language Listserv) 130, 151, 153
   on classroom layouts and classroom
    management techniques 31
   Fluency First 153
   moderated list 154
text editor
   and browser run together 136
   to make webpages 134–5
theme, activities by 38
time 85–7, 95–6
time capsule 132
time differences, and speed of access 3
timetables 95–6
titles, finding 28
translation, of webpages 22
travel 61–2, 69–71, 71–3, 84–5, 87–8, 95–6,
   100–1
Tripod 141
truncation, in searches 22
TUCOWS 135, 161

underlining, in webpages 139
updating, websites 33
used to 48–9
user identification, software which requires
   34

video 32, 148, 149
video-conferencing 3
virus protection software 16, 34
virus warning, via email 16
vocabulary
   books and reading 66–7
   cinema 57–9, 88–90
   clothes and fashion 93–5
   computers 39–41
   food 79–80
   holiday 61–2
   housing 115–16
   music 46–7

news 56–7
parties and celebrations 100–1
revision 98–9
sports 82–3
television 59–60
travel 71–3
weather 53–4, 101–3
Web *see* World Wide Web
Web browsers *see* browsers
Web-based projects 134–47
Webcrawler 27
webpage design 135
webpages 5
   adding an image 138–9
   adding hypertext links 140–1
   addresses 6, 9, 12
   changing document colours 140
   class project 144–5
   click and drag a selection of text for a
    worksheet 9
   file names 141
   formatting 139–40
   increasing space for 161
   making simple 134–47
   project tips 147
   putting them on the Internet 141
   sample projects 142–7
   scrolling up and down 8
   seeing how they have been made via *Source*
    140
   tips for making 141–2
   translation of 22
websites 6, 8
   bilingual 143
   corporate 30
   FAQs 8–9
   frames 9
   length of life 33
   page caching 32–3
   planning on paper 142
   reviewing 126–7, 170–1
   saving for future reference 18
   updating 33
Word 4, 9, 15, 134
word processing skills, basic 9, 30
word processing software, to make webpages
   134–5
work conditions, discussions of 153
worksheets
   sample 37
   using part of a webpage for 9
world problems 103–4
World Wide Web 3–8
   defined 5
   FAQs 8–9
   your first visit 6–8

9855

WriteNow! 133
writing
    projects 133–4
    and publishing 105–6
WWW *see* World Wide Web

Xoom 141

Yahoo! 6, 17–18
    compared with *AltaVista* 24–5
    subject guide 23–5
young learners
    activities for 37
    groups for teachers of 153
    introduction to the Internet 27